Netivot Shalom

Insights on the Holidays and *Avoda*
Based on the Writings of the Slonimer Rebbe

MAGGID

Rabbi Yitzchok Adlerstein

Netivot
Shalom

**Insights on the Holidays and *Avoda*
Based on the Writings of the Slonimer Rebbe**

Maggid Books

Netivot Shalom
Insights on the Holidays and Avoda
Based on the Writings of the Slonimer Rebbe

First Edition, 2019

Maggid Books
An imprint of Koren Publishers Jerusalem Ltd.

POB 8531, New Milford, CT 06776-8531, USA
& POB 4044, Jerusalem 9104001, Israel
www.maggidbooks.com

© Yitzchok Adlerstein, 2019

The publication of this book was made possible through the generous
support of *Torah Education in Israel* and *The Jewish Book Trust Inc.*

ISBN 978-1-59264-535-0, *hardcover*

A CIP catalogue record for this title is
available from the British Library

Printed and bound in the United States

אשר זעליג וייס
כגן 8
פעיה"ק ירושלם ת"ו

ב"ה   ז' אדר ע"ב

לפני מספר שנים יצא לאור ספר "תבין לחידות" מלאכת מעשה ידיו להתפאר של ידידי יקירו איש רב רוח בו חכם ושובר הרב יצחק וולפשטיין הי"ו. בספר זה פירק ובאר קושיות ומאמרים של מרן בעל הגאון בעל בחידות אלו לעת בהנגלות.

ספר זה נחשב שורש כספר יסוד למשנת הנשמות ומקומה, ורבות מוסבים בו תציר כמי למתבונן על קבלה ומקום הקודש. כעת באנגלית נתגדל והגדיל והאדיר את תוכנו בהיקף ובהסברים של ספר זה לקוראי שפה זו.

ועתה זוכה להוציא חלק ב' כעניני בקודשים ומצוות המקדש. ומה נאה ומה נכון רק גדולה דקדוקי, ספר נפלא וזה ונשאלתי קרבים אותנו לאור ויתעלם על ידו.

על כן מברך אני שיזכה תמיד להגדיל תורה ולהאדירה ולבוא הגאולה של גמורה ימצא לו ולכל ביתו שמחה ושלום ונחת.

הכותב וחותם

אשר זעליג וייס
אב"ד
וראש ישיבת
"דרכי תורה"
פעיה"ק ירושלים ת"ו

Asher Zelig Weiss
Kagan 8
Jerusalem

Iyar 5779

Several years ago, the first volume of "*Understanding Netivot*" was published thanks to the efforts of "a man of spirit," my wise and esteemed friend Rabbi Yitzchok Adlerstein. This book provides English interpretation and explanation of lessons from the honored and holy Rebbe, author of *Netivot Shalom*. This book has become known as a fundamental source for understanding Hasidic ideas and the service of God, and many have studied it in order to draw near to Him. Rabbi Adlerstein has succeeded in conveying the deep and wonderful content of this book for English speakers.

Now he has devoted the second volume to the topics of the holidays and the foundations of *avodat Hashem*. As was the first, so is the second – this is a wonderful book guaranteed to enlighten and strengthen many.

May the author *shlit"a* always merit to increase Torah, and may the great merit of *Netivot Shalom* uphold him and his family with joy, peace, and truth.

Fondly,
Asher Zelig Weiss

In loving memory of my dear Father

Lionel A. Walpin, M.D. *z"l*

אריה לייב אברהם בן אליעזר יהושע ז"ל

He was a gifted physician, musician, innovator and teacher.
His love for family, Judaism, and Israel is an inspiration
to his grandchildren and great-grandchildren.

Dr. Loren Greenberg

In honor of our father, Rabbi Yitzchok Adlerstein, an eminent scholar and original thinker, who has nurtured and developed creative thought and intellectual honesty in every one of his children. One of his favorite means of transmitting these lessons has been through his renowned and sometimes "out-of-the-box" *parsha* questions at the Shabbos table, often based on the *Nesivos Shalom*. While maintaining that every thought and idea must be deeply examined and not blindly accepted, he always managed to show us how the Torah is the true source of all wisdom. He continues to influence the next generation, his grandchildren, who have already grown to appreciate his genuine love of Torah…and difficult *parsha* questions.

Abba, we are forever grateful to you for opening our minds and enabling us to comprehend the depth and greatness of Torah, strengthening us as individuals in a complex world, to become independent thinkers with the Torah as our guiding light. Of course, none of this would have been possible without the gentle love, support, and insight we all received from your *eishes chayil*, our dear and beloved mother, who has always been there to embrace anyone looking to gain from your knowledge, bridging all cultural and social differences and creating an atmosphere conducive to open discussion and growth.

Thank you for making the teachings of the *Nesivos Shalom* a real part of our lives. In your endeavor to bring the beauty of the *Nesivos Shalom* to the general public, you empower multitudes with its refreshing and relevant ideas, enabling them to benefit in much the same way as we have. May you continue to use your strengths and influence to respond to those who challenge, to guide those who yet search, and to inspire all of us – no matter which lane we travel on the *Derech HaTorah*, the superhighway whose parallel lanes are all *Nesivos Shalom*, paths of peace.

With love and admiration,
Your children

Contents

Introduction

W hat keeps the world going?" asks the Gemara at the end of Sota.[1] Having established that the destruction of the *Beit HaMikdash* threw the world into an ever-worsening decline, the Gemara indicates that something must provide sufficient resistance to the process to prevent the world from collapsing entirely.

The world endures, answers the Gemara, "upon the *Kedusha* of the Order (*Kedusha DeSidra*) and upon the response of 'May His great name be blessed' of the Aggada." This *Kedusha* of the Order, Rashi explains, is the *kedusha* that was added to the very end of the morning prayer, which includes an elaboration of its meaning in Aramaic. In effect, it is a short exercise in Torah learning that is shared by all of Israel, the schooled and the unschooled together. In this brief moment every day[2] was a nexus of Torah study and *kiddush Hashem*, sanctification of God's name. Similarly, the public gathered on Shabbat to listen to words of Aggada – the homiletical explication of the Torah. When the crowd

---

1. Sota 49a.
2. See *Beit Yosef, Oraḥ Ḥayim* 132, according to which there was a longer order of verses and explanations on Shabbat, when people were not in as much of a hurry to exit the synagogue.

xiii

listened to the recitation of *kaddish* at the conclusion of the *derasha*, their mass response of "May His great name be blessed" also married Torah to *kiddush Hashem*. This combination is particularly cherished by God, and it allows the world to soldier on.

The works of Rav Shalom Noach Berezovsky *zt"l*, the Slonimer Rebbe, continue to captivate the Jewish world. They come closest to a contemporary example of a series of texts hungrily consumed by everyone: *Hassidim* and *mitnagdim; haredim* and Modern Orthodox; the schooled and the unschooled. The sheer number of people who turn to his words for illumination, inspiration, and a tried-and-true method of upgrading their personal relationships with the Almighty is a massive *kiddush Hashem*. Like the *Kedusha* of the Order, *Netivot Shalom* (the title of his main works) is at an uncommon nexus of Torah study and sanctifying God's name.

Netivot Shalom works because of the rare combination of gifts that the Rebbe brought to his position. He had studied in the Slonimer yeshiva Torat Hesed of Baranovitch, which blended a Hassidic approach with a Lithuanian one, as both its *rosh yeshiva* and *mashgiah* were rooted in the latter. He wrote with the warmth and passion of the Hassidic world, but expressed himself with the clarity of an accomplished *rosh yeshiva*, having founded one in Tel Aviv, after which he continued to lecture for five decades. He possessed the hands-on experience of a major rebbe; he knew of real people and the real issues they grappled with. He excelled in confronting the realities of modern life – especially the spiritual challenges and failings of people – with extraordinary honesty.

If one were able to design a person with all the right tools to lead and inspire the largest number of people, one would have nothing to add to the Rebbe.

Kedusha DeSidra did not only offer a fuller explanation of the verses of the *kedusha* – it offered it in the vernacular. As Meiri writes,[3] "That translation was comprehended by them, so that it was as if everyone was studying Torah." The rabbis of the Talmud understood that for the exercise to be truly universal, language could not be a barrier.

A number of years ago, I published an English-language adaptation of selections by the Rebbe from his five-volume work on Humash.

---

3. *Beit HaBehira* on Sotah 49a, s.v. *af al pi*.

My aim was to serve two audiences: those with insufficient language skills or background to study *Netivot Shalom* on their own, and those who have the skills but vastly prefer the quick access that an English-language work provides. I tried to stay faithful to the original, but tailored my adaptations to the needs of the Anglo world. I knew that certain kinds of arguments were likely to be less than persuasive, and that there were limitations of the length of what people would read.

That book was well received. In this new volume, I try to do much the same with material primarily from the other two volumes of *Netivot Shalom*. The material falls under two headings. One is the yearly calendar; the reader will find essays that make each special season or calendar day come alive in its unique spiritual meaning and potential. The second is a sampling of the Rebbe's treatment of different aspects of growth in *avodat Hashem* – the science of learning how to serve Hashem more meaningfully.

This book should serve in the merit of my mother-in-law, Devora Ita (Aviva) Metchik, *a"h*, who took leave of this existence for a better destination while the book was in preparation, and who provided me with my most important asset in writing and in life: my dear wife Reena, *amu"sh.*

Lehavdil bein ḥayim leḥayim, it should also serve in the merit of the family members who are the most meaningful parts of my life. The list starts with my mother Trudy, *amu"sh*, and my father-in-law, Yitz-chok HaKohen Metchik, *amu"sh* – may they enjoy long life, health and happiness. It continues with our children Dovi and Rachel; Shevi and Rabbi Moshe; Yehuda and Chana; Rabbi Pesach and Malki; Yoni and Yehudis; Ari and Rebecca; Tzvi and Chani; Rabbi Akiva and Meira; and all of their children. May we all see the unending *naḥat* of בנים ובני בנים נאמנים להשם ולתורתו.

Grateful thanks go to sponsors known and unknown. Perhaps at publication, I will find out who some of them are.

While I had a rough manuscript in hand, this book would not have come about without the encouragement, assistance and expertise of the professionals at Koren Publishers. Here, as well, I do not know the identity of all, but wish to thank them anyway. Some I can thank by name: Matthew Miller, publisher of Maggid Books; Rabbi Reuven

Ziegler, whose enthusiasm for publishing is singularly driven by his passion for Torah; and the editorial team of Debbie Ismailoff, Ita Olesker, and Shira Finson.

I could not have produced this work (and the several other incomplete manuscripts lying in wait) without the support of my superiors and colleagues at the Simon Wiesenthal Center of Los Angeles: Rabbi Moshe Hier, Rabbi Abraham Cooper, Rabbi Meyer May, and Evy and John Nelson. Through them, I have been able to tell myself that besides having the opportunity to contribute spiritually to the Jewish people, I am able professionally to be part of the small army of people who labor constantly on the political level to help our embattled people.

The greatest change in life in decades came with our move to Jerusalem, where we have finally come home. It was the dream of a lifetime – one that the people who knew us best thought we would never actualize. We weren't running from anything; to the contrary, we could not have made the move without the strength supplied by all our friends in Los Angeles, especially at Beis Midrash Kehilas Yaakov, and its *mara de'atra*, Rav Gershon Bess, *shlit"a*. We miss all of you. Of course, an extra measure of thanks goes to two of our children in Israel, Shevi and Peysi, who did all the heavy lifting for us to make the move a piece of cake. There is no way to thank you properly.

Mori verabbi HaGaon Rav Asher Weiss, *shlit"a*, made it easy to navigate the complex issues of *halakha* and general orientation that are part of making *aliyah*. Not only has he always been available, but he has been a constant source of warmth and encouragement. I sought only one approbation for this volume, and it was from him. Many thanks to him for providing it.

Neither is there a way to thank *HaKadosh Baruch Hu* for all the myriad *ḥassadim* that He has bestowed upon us in the years of our lives, and in the preparation of this book. In classic Jewish style, thanking Him always morphs into asking for more, and I will not break with tradition.

יהי רצון מלפני ה׳ שלא תמוש התורה מפי ומפי זרעי וזרע זרעי עד עולם.

Avoda

Avoda: A Primer

The Gemara's depiction[1] of the *oved Hashem*, the servant of God, does not give us much cause for celebration. Most of us will have to concede that we are not even close.

Here is what the Gemara says: "'You will return and see the difference between a righteous person and a wicked person, between one who serves God, and one who does not serve Him.'[2] .... There is no comparison between one who studies his passage one hundred times and one who studies his passage one hundred and one times." Most of us will have dropped out well before we approach the one hundredth time. Can that one last repetition be all that important?

This is the point. We cannot imagine ourselves getting too excited about the hundred and first round of studying anything at all. The novelty, the sense of discovery would have disappeared long before, leaving mostly tedium in its wake. That is precisely the idea. *Avodat Hashem*, the service of God, means first and foremost serving Him for the sole purpose of fulfilling His will, even when unaccompanied by any pleasure or

---

Based on *Netivot Shalom* 1:235–238.
1. Ḥagiga 9b.
2. Mal. 3:18.

positive feeling. The Gemara provides a hypothetical illustration regarding someone who might still squeeze some surprise and enjoyment from his one hundredth attempt at a piece of text but gets none at all from the one that follows. He makes that last attempt only because he believes God asks it of him. This makes him an *oved Hashem*. All his previous effort will be justly rewarded – but the toil alone does not entitle him to be called a servant of God.

We reach the level of *oved Hashem* only through the expenditure of extraordinary effort in fulfilling His will, even when unattended by any other satisfaction. We find this most pointedly in regard to Moshe Rabbenu. He is described as having qualities not shared by any other human being: speaking "mouth to mouth... beholding the image of God;"[3] "Never again has there arisen in Israel a prophet like Moshe, whom God had known face-to-face."[4] Yet it is neither of these extraordinary descriptions that capture his uniqueness and specialness but a much simpler one. When summing him up in an economy of words, the Torah calls him simply, "Moshe, the servant of God."[5] This title underscores his love for God, which allows him to do His bidding in the manner of a faithful servant.

The image is further amplified in a midrash.[6] A king decides to test the devotion of his children and servants. He wishes to distinguish between those who both fear and love him and those who only fear him but do not love him. He readies a narrow alley of four cubits by four cubits. Inside it, he constructs a courtyard of only four handbreadths on a side; it in turn contains an extremely narrow doorway. The king's children and servants stand within the alley and courtyard. He understands that only those who truly love him will push themselves through the doorway, will force themselves through with great exertion, and will thereby find the king on the other side.

Our Sages had this in mind when they declared, "[One who says] 'I toiled and succeeded' – believe him; 'I did not toil and succeeded' – do

---

3. Num. 12:8.
4. Deut. 34:10.
5. Josh. 1:1.
6. *Tanna DeVei Eliyahu* 16.

not believe him."[7] A person who attempts to apprehend God using his natural gifts and talents will not succeed, even if those gifts of intelligence and insight usually afford him penetrating insight and understanding. In reaching out across the abyss of incomprehension to God Himself, only toil and effort will be met with success.

This, then, is the requisite first step in the service of God: becoming a willing soldier, faithfully manning his assigned, holy station, and working with great effort. The *oved Hashem* is consistent in his performance, acting with the same alacrity during the dark times of his life as during the bright ones. Even when times seem oppressive to him – whether because he bears the load of weighty temptations and desires, or because his spirit is so darkened and uninspired that he feels that his entire facility for spiritual responsiveness has rotted away from within – he does not relent in fulfilling his obligations. He tells himself that if it is God's will that he live a spiritually darkened experience, then he will respond to that will with joy and happiness.

Acquiring this first step has prerequisites of its own. Chief among them is developing utter and complete confidence that victory is his if he wants it. He must know that if he struggles mightily and begins to push himself through the narrow doorway, God will help pull him the rest of the way. He must understand that God does not come after people cunningly.[8] If He challenges a person with extraordinary tests, He also gives that person extraordinary tools and talents to be able to pass those tests. A person must keep in mind that all the effort he is required to expend pales in comparison to what he will achieve – that of all the pleasures in this world, nothing holds a candle to the feeling of being close to God. Nothing could be a more worthwhile and profitable endeavor. He must hold to a steady course, never wavering, remembering the image of the Menora, literally monolithic, one continuous piece of pure gold, hammered into shape. Such must be his *avoda* – continuous and uninterrupted, knowing that any small break will weaken the entire enterprise.

You will come across people who have spent decades in pursuit of spirituality and are bitter and disappointed. Despite many years of trying,

---

7. Megilla 6b.
8. Avoda Zara 3a.

their achievement still comes up short. These people are often victims of their own enthusiasm. They have given valiantly of themselves – but skimped on the essential preparation. Working toward spirituality without first preparing oneself in the service of God simply does not work. It is the equivalent of spending lavishly on a tall building but doing an inadequate job on the underground foundation. A building will never last without a strong foundation. Understandably, there is some natural resistance to spending freely on the foundation – no one ever sees it. Such a policy, however, is foolish and counterproductive. Yet people do the same, jumping into the work of the seemingly more rewarding parts of the pursuit of spirituality without doing their due diligence in the very first and most important step – acquiring a strong commitment to *avodat Hashem*.

"Counterproductive" is not too strong a word. Our Sages tell us[9] that whoever wisdom exceeds his positive activities, his wisdom will not last. Would it not have been more accurate to refer to someone whose actions do not keep up with his wisdom? The problem cannot be his excess of knowledge so much as his deficiency of mitzvot!

Yet this is precisely the point. The Rebbe of Ruzhin offered the analogy of a fruit. God prepared the skin to protect the delicate tissue. If the tissue bulged and extended outside of the skin, many hazards would compromise the fruit's integrity. Wisdom requires the protection of significant mitzvot. Those mitzvot protect the integrity of the wisdom – of Torah learning and spiritual insight. Without protection, the wisdom itself is subject to attack by many waiting spiritual hazards which can bring great spiritual illness to a person.

It takes a bit of insight to realize how important the service of God is as the ground floor in spiritual progress. It takes more insight to sustain the task of building that sense of *avoda*, of accepting the responsibility of fulfilling God's will regardless of how much or how little fulfillment it may initially provide us. As in many areas of life, however, there are no shortcuts.

---

9. Mishna Avot 3:12.

It All Begins with *Ḥesed*

Hesed – loosely translated as "loving-kindness" but encompassing a much broader spectrum of compassionate behavior – is chief among good *middot*, good character traits. It is also the central principle around which all other principles of creation are predicated. All elements of *ḥesed* contribute to the upbuilding of the world; all forms of cruelty give rise to destructiveness.

Things could have been different, claimed the brother of the Maharal.[1] "*Olam ḥesed yibaneh*"[2] – the world will be built upon *ḥesed*. There is no *a priori* reason why this had to be. God could have chosen one of His other *middot* and spun a world revolving around it. He chose *ḥesed* because it is closest to His will. Similarly, when we are instructed to imitate God's *middot* (as fulfillment of the imperative "You shall walk in His ways"[3]), our Sages limit this obligation to the

---

Based on *Netivot Shalom* 1:98–100.

1. *Sefer HaḤayim.*
2. Ps. 89:3. Although the verse literally means "Forever will your kindness be built," it is often used the way it is above to illustrate the centrality of *ḥesed*.
3. Deut. 28:9.

midda of *ḥesed*, but no other.[4] It is through *ḥesed* alone that we can attach ourselves to Him.

We can perform acts of *ḥesed* with our property and ourselves. Greater still is when we rise to the level of becoming the very embodiment of *ḥesed* – when we become people of *ḥesed*. We then share in the Torah's description of Avraham, the quintessential person of *ḥesed*. About him the Torah writes, "And you will be a blessing."[5] This means, say our Sages, that anyone who was touched by Avraham or who dealt with him or even saw him was blessed, because Avraham himself had become a blessing. Indeed, the true person of *ḥesed* feels for the other and gives him his entire heart. When his friend is racked by pain and his spirit collapses within him, the *ḥesed* personality joins with him in his struggle, as stated in the verse, "I am with him in his trouble."[6] Conversely, at times of his friend's joy, he also stands with him as a partner.

The *ḥesed*-person influences all who enter his orbit. He gives everyone his attention, because he loves every Jew as himself. An aura of love and fraternity accompanies him; it seems as if his entire being is given over to assist the other. The *ḥesed*-person's being is shaped by the special nature of *ḥesed*, which is *hitpashtut*.[7] Thus, *ḥesed* and love emanate and extend from him, reaching both near and far. By contrast, the person who lacks *ḥesed* is, by nature, contracted and limited. He contains his capacity to love narrowly within and applies it only to himself.

Besides all of this, an added benefit is attached to this character trait. When a Jew conducts himself in the spirit of *ḥesed*, Heaven deals with him with the aforementioned *midda*. The Baal Shem Tov and other scholars emphasized that God relates to people according to the *middot* with which they live their lives. If they practice cruelty, the attribute of God's judgment is aroused against them, regardless of the validity of their

---

4. See, similarly, Maharal, *Netiv Gemilut Ḥasadim*, ch. 1, and *Paḥad Yitzḥak*, Rosh HaShana 31:4–6, 15.
5. Gen. 12:2.
6. Ps. 91:15.
7. Spreading, or extension. Some *middot* are focused narrowly, usually inwardly. Others – especially *ḥesed* – force the person to extend his ego, his focus, to the world beyond himself.

justification. The Maharal[8] shows at length that when a person attaches himself to the goodness of God by directing some of it to others, God directs some of that very good to the person himself.

Rabbi Avraham Weinberg in *Yesod HaAvoda* writes that a person should view an opportunity to do *ḥesed* as if he found great treasure. The Rebbe of Kobrin points out that exercising such an opportunity is a key to successful living. A day in which a Jew does not perform some favor or kindness for another, he taught, is a day not really lived.

One who diligently studies Torah but does not occupy himself with acts of *ḥesed* "is as if he did not have a God."[9] What he lacks, explains Rashi, is God protecting him. Were he to practice *ḥesed* as well as participate in Torah study, his affairs would be conducted from heaven through protocols of *ḥesed*. Thus, his umbrella of protection would be more complete, working to assure his safety even when he does not otherwise deserve to be spared.

Tikkun – the long process of bringing a flawed world back to the rarified state of Gan Eden before Adam's sin – began with Avraham. He started the process of reestablishing spiritual order to a world of chaos, of *tohu vavohu*[10], followed by the Six Shepherds that exemplified other *middot*.[11]

His contribution, of course, was the perfection of the *midda* of *ḥesed*. *Ḥesed* is associated with no figure in the Torah as strongly as with Avraham. Why, then, does *ḥesed* not appear on the mishna's[12] short list of characteristics of Avraham's disciples? Instead, the mishna speaks of a generous eye, a humble spirit, and a meek soul.

We might answer that when the mishna speaks of disciples of Avraham, it refers to Avrahams-in-training – those who aspire to become like him. The mishna does not describe Avraham the individual so much as how a person should position himself to be able to imitate his great

---

8. *Netivot Olam, Netiv Gemilut Ḥasadim*, ch. 3.

9. Avoda Zara 17b.

10. Gen. 1:2.

11. Avraham and these six others are known in Kabbala as the Seven Shepherds, more familiar to us as the *Ushpizin*, the spiritual guests in the sukka. Each corresponds to one of the seven lower *sefirot*.

12. Mishna Avot 5:22.

ḥesed. The three traits mentioned by the mishna are the important precursors to *ḥesed* activity. Nothing allows the natural *ḥesed* within us to flower and flourish as much as diminishing one's sense of self. Similarly, when the mishna describes the polar opposite traits and links them to Bilam, it assigns the blame for stunted *ḥesed* development to a heightened sense of self. The greatest barrier to acts of true *ḥesed* is *anokhiyut*, or selfishness.

This analysis is appealing but doesn't stand up to scrutiny. The facts indicate otherwise. We note much *ḥesed* performed by people who are not exemplars of the three traits of the mishna.

We need not discard our explanation, however. We can resolve the conflict with a simple but hugely important distinction. The mishna speaks of those who wish to become *ḥesed* personalities, whose *ḥesed* flows from their essential self. Acts of *ḥesed* can be done for reasons both more and less laudable. People who have not yet become full *ḥesed* personalities can be moved by circumstances to respond with *ḥesed*.

Only special people personify *ḥesed*, with *ḥesed* at their cores. We will discuss this further in future chapters.

Ḥesed as Vocation

Performing acts of *ḥesed* is wonderful, but it does not automatically turn one into a *ḥesed* personality.

While one who performs acts of *ḥesed* responds compassionately to anyone who needs it, he does not seek out new situations to which he can bring his *ḥesed*. But the person whose core is suffused with *ḥesed* will chase after charitable acts. He stands ready to sacrifice the material – and even the spiritual – in order to do *ḥesed* for others.

A midrash[1] has God chiding Iyyov. "You sit comfortably in your house, and guests come to you. You have not achieved half the measure of Avraham's *ḥesed*! He goes about seeking out guests."

The Torah depicts the *ḥesed* of Avraham in full blossom. Weak and in pain, three days after circumcision at an advanced age, he was free of any obligation to toil in the service of others. Concerned for his comfort, God created a heat wave that would protect him from bother. Instead, Avraham was pained because he could not serve guests, and sat expectantly, waiting for their arrival. The presence of the *Shekhina*, the Divine Presence, and the opportunity to converse with the Divine

---

Based on *Netivot Shalom* 1:100–101.

1. *Avot deRabbi Natan*, ch. 7 s.v. *veyihiyu aniyim*.

Presence were not sufficient to keep Avraham from his guests. He left the *Shekhina* behind, as it were, and ran to greet his guests, forever teaching us that offering proper hospitality to guests is more important than receiving the Divine Presence.

Avraham paid no attention to the identities of the recipients of his largesse. It made no difference to him if they were righteous people or idolatrous Arabs. No external factor, no perceived need, stimulated his interested in giving. His propensity for *ḥesed* presented itself constantly, at all times. If no one nearby presented himself as a recipient of his kindness, he would search out some other recipient. Avraham directed it even toward those who opposed what he stood for; he fervently prayed for the evildoers of the city of Sodom.[2]

Acting kindly to someone who needs assistance very often unwittingly causes some pain or discomfort to the recipient. Within our nature is a sense of shame in taking what we have not earned or deserved. Avraham's acts of *ḥesed* avoided this pitfall. Notice how many times he spoke to his guests as if they were doing him a favor by joining him: "Please, if I have found favor in your eyes; please do not pass by your servant."[3] He turned to the travelers, fatigued and thirsty in the brutal heat, and spoke to them as if they would be performing an act of kindness by joining him. He inverted the roles of benefactor and beneficiary, making himself the recipient and his guests the givers.

Eliezer's test of a potential match for Yitzḥak that he conducted by the well made use of this distinction between performing acts of *ḥesed* and the *ḥesed* personality. He would not be satisfied if a young lady offered to provide him with water; a compassionate person might very well volunteer such assistance. He was looking for something more than that. The response of the *ḥesed* personality moves beyond this; it was this that Eliezer considered crucial. Eliezer's request to Rivka implied that he needed water and nothing else – that he would be quite comfortable with water alone. The *ḥesed* personality is unperturbed by the lack of

---

2. According to the Sages, not only were they evil, but part of their evil was an utter rejection of *ḥesed*, Avraham's defining characteristic. They thus legislated against the performance of acts of kindness to strangers.

3. Gen. 18:3.

need and finds other places to direct the quest to give. Rivka impressed Eliezer precisely because she volunteered to water the camels as well, despite Eliezer having made no mention of it.

Opportunities to perform charitable acts envelop every aspect of a person's life – his property, his body, his house, and his soul. Performing acts of *ḥesed* with one's property includes giving *tzedaka* to the poor, extending support to one who has come upon hard times, and lending money to one in need. The act of refraining from lending money – even in the face of the cancellation of the debt through the approaching *Shemitta* year – is called a "base"[4] deed. However, the Torah warns against performing these monetary mitzvot with imperfect intent. "Do not find it evil in your heart when you give."[5] We are encouraged to give with positive intentions.

Performing acts of *ḥesed* with our bodies concerns us in two discrete ways. On the one hand, we are commanded to physically perform a variety of mitzvot including visiting the sick, burying the dead, unloading and loading distressed animals, returning lost property. Within these commandments, however, we discern another level of *ḥesed*. We should ready our bodies in anticipation of the performance of acts of *ḥesed*, so that we will jump into service with the eagerness of one who is collecting rare treasure.

Performing acts of *ḥesed* with our homes affords us the opportunity to turn them entirely into mitzva objects, sanctifying them entirely to God. Offering hospitality allows us to perform charitable acts to rich and poor alike, as opposed to *tzedaka*, which by definition must restrict itself to the poor.

Being hospitable to guests, as our Sages tell us and as we see with Avraham, is greater than receiving the Divine Presence. A simple analogy explains this. Imagine a good friend appearing on your door step unannounced. If he is a dear friend, you will react with unrestrained joy in seeing him and lavish all kinds of attention upon him. Could anything demonstrate warmth and closeness more than such a reception?

Yes, indeed. Imagine the son of your friend – an individual you have never met or spoken with before – arriving in a similar manner. If you receive him with the same enthusiasm and alacrity as you would

---

4. Deut. 15:9.
5. Ibid. 15:10.

his father, you have made a powerful statement. He returns to his father and relates the happiness that greeted him and the royal treatment that he received when people discovered that he was the son of their dear friend. The father's satisfaction is even greater when this unknown and unrecognized son of his is so graciously received.

Every Jew is a prince, the son of the King. When a Jews welcomes some unknown and unrecognized son of the King, he brings great satisfaction to the Father. We multiply the value of the gracious reception when the guests are Torah scholars or people who have done great deeds who continue their holy work from within our homes. When we do so, we combine acts of *ḥesed* with serving God.

The greatest form of *ḥesed* we can perform takes place internally, within our deepest thoughts. When a friend is broken and in anguish, we can go beyond showing that we take part in his pain – we can identify with the pain so completely that we experience it as our own.

There is no greater support we can offer another than taking on his pain as an equal partner. Sharper than any physical pain or financial loss is the mental pain and loneliness that comes with feeling that no one understands his situation or stands with him. The true *ḥesed* personality will find a way to demonstrate his solidarity at such a time, showing himself to be a caring brother, encouraging the individual in pain and supporting him, breathing into him new life with the belief that God will care for him and that there will be an end to the darkness.

This kind of *ḥesed* is a fulfillment of two mitzvot. We are commanded to "walk in His ways,"[6] to imitate God's *middot* of *ḥesed* and mercy. It follows that we are obligated to commiserate with a person in pain, even when he will not respond or even know the depth of our feeling. We must do it to attach ourselves to God's trait of compassion. Additionally, part of the basic level of loving another as ourselves[7] is to resist and fight any pain suffered by another. We cannot do that without first understanding the pain and only then battling against it.

6. Deut. 28:9.
7. Lev. 19:18.

Prayer: Front and Center

What would we not give to trade the poverty of our spiritual lives for the company of Rabbi Ḥayim Vital and his generation? Yet his depiction[1] of the spiritual level of the people of his time leaves us wondering whether he was looking at us when he composed it. "An atmosphere of coarseness has taken hold of our times. Through it, heresy abounds. Left to our own devices, we routinely fail to stand up to the evil inclination. Because the *nefesh*[2] – the lowest of the three parts of the soul[3] – is tightly linked to and mired in the physical body, sin seems inescapable."

We can be sure that the shortcomings he mourned pale by comparison to what we deal with in our communities. His forecast, therefore, should be met by us with even greater foreboding. And we certainly should hang on to every word of his prescription for change.

Based on *Netivot Shalom* 1:180, 188–191.

1. *Etz Ḥayim*, introduction.
2. Typically, the part of the soul that mediates action and is therefore implicated in the active transgressions.
3. The other two elements that are accessible to most people are *ruaḥ* and *neshama*.

Rabbi Vital was confident that there must be an exit strategy to release us from the vise-like grip of the evil inclination. He found it in praying with concentration and focus. Today it remains our best strategy in more spiritually impoverished times.

The *Beit Avraham* fleshes out the thought for us. Prayer is called *avoda shebalev,* the service of the heart. The word *avoda* generally alludes to the work of coaxing sustenance from the ground. Before the earth yields anything of value, we must perform three activities. We first plow and ready the soil, then we plant and sow, and finally we water.

Praying properly requires the same three processes. First, we plow through the accumulated underbrush of our minds, opening our hearts to prayer. Next, we plant words of prayer within our hearts. Finally, we drench those words with the tears of our fervent entreaties to God.

Prayer is successful because it offers the antidote to our evil inclination at the point of entry through which it could gain a foothold within us. Most of our spiritual undoing lies in our lusts and desires. Prayer allows us to direct those selfsame desires to God Himself. The *Beit Avraham* describes how we do this, employing the words of verses that are familiar to us. "Hashem, my God, I cried out to You and You healed me."[4] Crying out to God in prayer is itself the largest measure of the healing we seek. Through it, we substitute God Himself for the usual objects of desire of the soul and flesh. "My soul thirsts for You; my flesh longs for You"[5] ultimately reaches a point of "My heart and my flesh sing to the living God."[6] Whereas we may feel sinful in our very bones, prayer changes our attitude to "All my bones will say, 'God, who is like You?'" In place of the faintness we feel from head to toe, we are invigorated through prayer, until we say, "Every eye shall look toward You; every knee shall bend to You; every erect spine shall prostrate itself before You; all the hearts shall fear You; all innermost feelings and thoughts shall sing praises to Your name."

Prayer must become an experience akin to immersion in a *mikve,* albeit a *mikve* of fire. Similar to the laws of purging utensils of non-kosher

---

4. Ps. 30:3.
5. Ibid. 63:2.
6. Ibid. 84:3.

absorption, where items used through fire are purged through fire, our fiery desires within us can be purged only through the heated intensity of our praying.

We know that the three daily prayers correspond to the order of the *korbanot*, or offerings, that were offered in the Temple.[7] Closeness to God is the all-important central pillar of our service; in turn, the blandishments of the evil inclination are chiefly aimed at separating a Jew from his holy Source and creating a wedge of distance where only union should exist. Sacrifices were aimed at restoring the closeness. (The Maharal[8] points out that the word *korban* derives from the word *karov*, or close.)

Some transgressions were largely products of the evening hours. If a Jew stumbled in one of them, say our Sages,[9] the daily morning offering would restore his equilibrium. Other transgressions belonged to the daytime activities; the daily afternoon offering would address them. In the evening, we were often left with our higher-order selves fatigued or completely dormant; what prevailed was our animal nature. The large limbs brought up to the altar to burn through the night dealt not with actual transgressions, but with the shortcomings owing to the coarser parts of our nature.

In all cases, it was the holy fire that burned constantly atop the altar that lit the fire of holiness within the Jewish people. That fire overpowered the evil fire of lower desires, and brought us back to where we belonged.

After the destruction of the Temple, the Sages ordained that the daily prayers should fulfill the role of the offerings. If we fail during the evening hours, we can pour out our hearts to God in the morning, during Shaharit, the morning prayer, and beg and entreat Him to be brought close once again. Minha, the afternoon prayer, affords us the same opportunity for our daytime failures. Maariv, the evening prayer, which the Gemara terms non-obligatory, or *reshut*, corresponds to our

---

7. Berakhot 26b.
8. *Netivot Olam, Netiv HaAvoda ch.3.*
9. Numbers Rabba 21:21.

shortcomings in the arena of permitted activities in which we overindulge, being contemptible with the permission of the Torah.

We find this correspondence between praying and the restoration of our closeness to God in early sources. Rabbenu Yona[10] writes: "*Korbanot* and prayer are of the same nature. A person draws closer to his Creator through them, enabling him to cling completely to Him, without any barrier intervening between them." Rabbi Yehuda HaLevi in the *Kuzari*[11] writes: "You should look with desire to the hour of prayer as the choicest of times of the day. At its time, a person becomes more like the spiritual beings and less like the animal ones. The three prayer periods provide food for the soul like physical food feeds the body."

A key motif of our prayer, therefore, must be our supplication to God when we find ourselves in difficult spiritual straits, i.e., when our hearts ache from our having moved away from Him; when we do not feel His closeness.

We have it on the authority of earlier Hasidic rebbes that no accusatory force stands in the way of a prayer for spiritual elevation and its heavenly address. Such forces sometimes block the way of other prayers – when we seek material benefits that we do not really deserve. There can be no such objections to seeking spiritual elevation. When we make the desire for closeness to God a key component of our prayer, we are assured that there is nothing but open highway between ourselves and the place we want our prayer to reach.

---

10. *Shaarei Teshuva, Shaarei Avoda,* section 8.
11. *Kuzari* 3:5.

How We Pray

The Rambam loses no time at the beginning of *Hilkhot Tefilla* in placing prayer in a mitzva universe of its own. Unlike so many practical, activity-oriented mitzvot, prayer is an *avoda*, a divine "service," albeit performed in the heart.

The Rambam proceeds to dissect this unique mitzva, but we are puzzled by some of the components. We find it difficult to understand why all of these pieces are so valuable in painting a spiritual canvas of praying. Why is the regularity so important – that we "pray and entreat each day"? Why is it essential that we "relate His praises"? And what is so spiritual and so essential about "asking for our needs… in requests and entreaties"? Why all the fuss? Prayer comes naturally to the believer. You need something – you ask for it! If and when a person is moved to ask for something, let him simply go to the One who can fill his request. Why do we elevate this practice into a complex and precisely structured spiritual exercise?

The Ari pithily observed that the holy intentions of praying bring about the union of God and His *Shekhina*. At the heart of this mystical teaching stands the very down-to-earth central element of

---

Based on *Netivot Shalom* 1:181–185.

prayer – prayer is about our union with God. This *devekut*, this state of utter attachment of a human soul to God, is so potent that it spills over to the upper worlds, where it brings the Holy One, blessed be He, and the *Shekhina* together in a mystical union.

When this realization penetrates, we have little trouble understanding all the details that the Rambam includes. Each one plays a role in bringing us close to God, in leading us to *devekut*.

First, the Rambam tells us that a person should "pray and entreat each day." He does not mean that we turn to God for our needs – he mentions that later. Rather, the Rambam tells us that the essence of praying is pouring out our souls from a heart full of love into the heart of the One we love. A more elevated subcategory of this emotional expression is pouring out our souls specifically about spiritual needs, whether they are born of intense longing for God or of the pain of feeling distant from Him. As mentioned above, this kind of prayer is particularly potent. When we ask Him for other things, we have no guarantee that our prayer will be accepted. Many demurrers in the heavenly courts can block our prayer. When we ask for pure spirituality, nothing stands in our way; our prayers are heard and answered.

The Rambam then speaks about declaring God's praise. This, too, is difficult to grasp at first. Of what value are the praises of puny, uncomprehending man, who cannot begin to understand the greatness of his Creator? Whatever words he offers actually diminish God's honor rather than add to it, because he so completely understates – no matter how hard he tries – God's greatness. (The Gemara[1] actually mocks the person who is lavish in his praise of God: "Have you completely accounted for *all* His praises?")

We can find an illuminating model in the singing of *shira*, or songs of praise, which is greatly lauded by our Sages. Why is it so valuable? Because these songs give expression to the closeness we feel for God. Its source is the longing for Him, the thirst for closeness that cannot be slaked. All ordinary praise of God in our praying can and should also spring from our *devekut* with Him.

---

1. Berakhot 33b.

The Maharal[2] explains even more. *Shira*, he says, is appropriate to the Jewish people because they are described as God's children. This means more than that we occupy a special place, as it were, in God's heart. Young children lead lives of complete dependence upon parents. They cannot assert independence in any meaningful way. Part of our being God's children is that we are able to recognize our absolute dependence on Him, to the exclusion of all other possibilities of support. There is no pretense of our being able to make it on our own.

Jews can be described as the "effects" gravitating to their Cause. The Maharal takes up this theme to explain the midrash that at the crossing of the Sea of Reeds, a nursing child turned away from its mother when it saw the *Shekhina*, and it, too, recited the Song of the Sea. Ordinarily, the bond between baby and mother is that of effect and cause. The child is completely dependent upon and linked to the mother, who both gave birth to him and continues to supply him with all his needs. When the *Shekhina* manifested itself at the Sea of Reeds, however, the child discovered his more fundamental Cause, and turned toward it in declaration of that dependence. This thought gives voice to the mode of address of the Jewish people to God in singing *shira*: a declaration of full and absolute dependence.

The statement of connection and dependence is not limited to joyous declaration through songs of praise. In truth, it applies to the opposite as well. Feelings of pain and suffering can also be a kind of song, in that they too can express profound longing for God. A person can sense God's love for him in the midst of, or more accurately, because of the suffering he endures. He can sense that God afflicts him only to lovingly guide him in a different direction.

Succinctly put, a person cannot sing any kind of *shira* with stunted, suppressed feelings, nor with a closed-up mind and heart. *Shira* can come only when emotions are unrestrained, allowing them to be developed and magnified.

When our emotions are set free in this way, the possibilities for songs of praise multiply. We then participate in these songs not only through expansiveness but even in our travail. To be sure, we recite a

---

2. *Gevurot Hashem*, ch. 47.

form of *shira* when we properly read from *Pesukei DeZimra*, the selections of praise in Psalms in the morning prayer: "Praise God from the heavens. Praise Him in the heights…. Praise Him, sun and moon; praise Him, all bright stars…. Praise God from the earth, sea giants and all watery depths. Fire and hail, snow and vapor, raging wind fulfilling His word."[3]

There is a form of *shira*, however, implicit as well when we address Him in a very different mood: "Hashem, do not rebuke me in Your anger, nor chastise me in Your rage. Favor me, Hashem, for I am feeble."[4] "How long, God, will you endlessly forget me? How long will You hide Your face from me?"[5] Both of these passages, despite their plaintive character, appear in sections of Psalms that are labeled *mizmor*, which is song, not lamentation. Even "O God, the nations have entered into Your inheritance; they have defiled the Sanctuary of Your holiness"[6] is part of a *mizmor*. For those who composed these lines, all was song. David found himself in the wilderness, far from the precincts of holiness, and through it expressed his longing for God: "O God, You are my God. I seek You. My soul thirsts for You. My flesh longs for You."[7] In the midst of his adversity, crying out to God whose closeness he sought was itself a form of song.

On Shabbat, we elevate this mode of praying to a position of exclusivity. We eliminate all the requests and petitions from the middle section of *Shemoneh Esreh* and instead wax lyrical about the specialness of Shabbat. During the week we spend ample time expressing our vulnerabilities, our wants and desires, and we directly beseech God for solutions. We also seek closeness to God through the song of praising Him. On Shabbat, when we taste of the experience of the World to Come, we elect only the more elevated of the two modes and shift entirely to giving voice to our longing and desire for Him. We act similarly on holidays, where the *Musaf* prayer speaks of our longing for Him in the midst

---

3. Ps. 148.
4. Ibid. 6:2–3.
5. Ibid. 13.
6. Ibid. 79:1.
7. Ibid. 63:1–2.

of our exile, without the closeness of the Temple. On the Days of Awe we are even more focused. We spend an enormous amount of time in *shira*, all of it effectively connected to one theme: our intense desire to see God's kingship reign fully over the entire world.

The Rambam continues with a third element of prayer, one we mentioned above in passing. We ask God for all we need. We might think that this is self-centered and unholy.[8]

The Maharal[9] explains that the opposite is true. By turning to God for every need, large and small, we negate our self-sufficiency and self-importance. Instead, we realize that we are utterly dependent upon Him and therefore inexorably attached to him, as surely as a tree is attached to the ground.

The daily schedule of prayer allows us to refine this idea of complete dependence, to experience it with all parts of our being.

In the first moments of consciousness, our basic physicality resists any suggestion of disturbing the sweetness and tranquility of sleep, or lying dormant and inactive. Rising to pray Shaharit, we submit ourselves physically to His service.

Sometime in the midst of our frenetic activity to wring as much productivity out of our working time as possible, we pause for Minha. In so doing, we attach our material interests entirely to Him.

After dark, when we contend with work-induced exhaustion, it is natural that we should want nothing more than calm, solitude, and rest. We disturb the stillness and serenity that we seek in our spirits by stopping once more and turning to God at Maariv. Having put our physical and monetary selves on hold for a few hours of the night, we thus commit what is left – our spiritual selves – to God.

Between the different daily prayers, then, we emphasize our complete reliance upon Him, holding back none of our different aspects – physical, monetary, or spiritual. In everything we are, we are really only Him and His will. This is the mature understanding of what we call

---

8. Indeed, newcomers to observance often voice their surprise that we attach so much spiritual significance to asking God to give us things.
9. *Netivot Olam, Netiv HaAvoda*, ch. 3.

Elokut. His Divinity means that He is the recognized, perceived power behind all of us and everything.

It is natural to look out for ourselves to satisfy our ordinary wants and desires. Each of us is at the center of our own universe. Nothing is as real to us as our own experience, because everything we think or know or sense exists within our own experience. According to this passage in Maharal, in our quest to look out for ourselves, we come to realize that we are not so real and not so central. We gradually understand that the ultimate reality, and the only ultimate existence, is God Himself.

Paradoxically, it is the part of prayer that seems most egocentric – our laundry list of needs and wants – that leads us to the conclusion that it is not about us at all.

An Introduction
to Inner Purity

Our Sages speak in such powerful and absolute terms about the importance of *middot*, character traits, that you might wonder if they are overstating their significance. When they look for a definite line in the sand differentiating "us" and "them," they turn to *middot*. ("Whoever possesses these three things – a generous eye, a humble spirit, a meek soul – is among the disciples of Avraham; whoever possesses ... [their opposite] is among the disciples of the wicked Bilam."[1]) When they paint a picture of the person who pleases his Creator, they again turn to *middot*. ("Whomever the spirit of the public finds pleasing, God finds pleasing."[2])

They are not exaggerating. Attaining excellent character traits is not just an important mitzva, incumbent upon every person to pursue. Rather, character traits are the person! They are foundational to the observance of Torah and mitzvot and fully determine whether or not

---

Based on *Netivot Shalom* 1:75–77.
1. Mishna Avot 5:19.
2. Ibid. 3:10.

a person can be said to have accomplished the task for which he was created. (If they are so important, asked Rabbi Ḥayim Vital in *Shaarei Kedusha*, why don't they appear on the list of the 613 mitzvot? The answer, he said, is that they are the all-important preparation for the mitzvot. In that sense, a deficiency in positive character traits is a more serious lapse than the failure to observe mitzvot!) Without proper character traits, taught Rabbenu Yona, Torah cannot take up residence within a person.[3] Sandwiched between a description of the attitudinal foundations of Torah belief and his detailed listing of all the practical laws of the Torah, the Rambam found it necessary to place his *Hilkhot De'ot*, describing the character traits that he saw as primary in the quest for mitzva fulfillment.

Good character traits are the wings with which a person takes spiritual flight. Without them, a person's Torah and mitzvot are not able to soar. To whatever extent a person perfects his character traits, his entire being is uplifted, raising his Torah and prayer to a higher plane. For this very reason the evil inclination shows unusual strength and tenacity in this arena. More so than in other areas, the evil inclination wishes to clip our wings, so that we cannot elevate ourselves. The teachers of the *Musar* movement, which taught a systematic approach to refining one's character, say that it is easier to become proficient in *Shas* than to uproot a single evil trait that has taken hold in our heart.

Good character is readily endorsed by most people. Those who show exemplary character traits win profuse praise from the masses. Teachers of *musar* are even more enthusiastic in describing the importance of character traits. To them, character traits are everything – they define the person. *Ḥasidut* provides the conceptual framework for building an even taller pedestal upon which to place proper character traits. *Ḥasidut* sees closeness to God as the objective of all Torah and mitzvot. Imperfect character traits simply do not allow that closeness and relationship – "the cursed cannot attach themselves to the blessed."[4]

---

3. Ibid. 3:17.
4. Rashi on Gen. 24:39.

In the way of *Ḥasidut*, acquiring superlative character traits is insufficient. A person must also extirpate the evil from within; he must change his very being so that these sterling character traits become part of his essence. As is stated in *Peri Haaretz*, what good is it that a person does not violate any transgressions if he has not erased the source of transgression from his heart?

The Gemara informs us about a survival tactic. "Whenever Yisrael [envelop themselves in a tallit as God demonstrated to Moshe and] perform the order of the thirteen *middot* [attributes of God], they are immediately answered."[5] *Reishit Ḥokhma*, however, cites those who find difficulty with this claim. Do we not see many people and communities reciting the thirteen *middot* without their prayers bringing them much success? The following answer is given: "Performing" here does not mean reciting. It means emulating those attributes of God and integrating them into their personalities.

Happiness is working on oneself and achieving pure character traits. Good character traits bring happiness; bad *middot* bring the opposite. The days of a person burdened by bad character traits are full of anger and bitterness. He consumes others and is consumed himself in the process. He is not tolerated by others nor can he tolerate the company of men. Thus his life ceases to be one worth living. One who is privileged to have purified his character traits, on the other hand, is always happy. He delights in others, and others delight in him. He is a source of blessing to himself and all around him. (This is what God meant when He told Avraham, "And you will be a blessing."[6]

The Rambam provides a startling anecdote[7] about perfected *middot*.

A Hasid was asked, "What was the happiest day of your life?" This is what he answered: "I traveled by boat. My place on the vessel was the least desirable, lowliest of all. One of the passengers saw

---

5. Rosh HaShana 17b. The thirteen *middot* refer to that number of God's characteristics listed in Ex. 34:6–7.
6. Gen. 12:2.
7. Commentary to Mishna Avot 4:4.

me as so insignificant and degraded that he relieved himself upon me. By the life of God – I was not pained by what he did, and my anger did not rise within me. I was overjoyed that the disgrace did not pain me, and that I did not sustain any hurt from it."

Another person would have seen that day as the worst imaginable, being treated in such a disgraced manner. The Hasid saw his achievement of ultimate forbearance as grounds for ecstasy.

The recipe for success in character development includes an ingredient not immediately recognizable as part of the character trait orbit. Ultimately, all issues of good and evil revolve around a single central point: holiness. No one can perfect his character without having incorporated holiness in his life. As the Ramban[8] explains, the call to holiness includes what is permissible according to halakha that has not been proscribed by the Torah. Holiness means elevating the arena of *reshut*, those things and activities that are neither forbidden nor mandatory.

The two must work in tandem. We work on perfecting our inner character traits while endeavoring to increase the holiness of the way we live our lives. Keeping both of these goals before us, we can hope to "ascend the mountain of Hashem."[9]

---

8. Lev. 19:2.
9. Ps. 24:3.

Holiness Is Not Optional

I t makes no sense. Why do people who pride themselves on meticulousness in observance, people who take upon themselves all sorts of stringencies in the practice of the law, nonetheless ignore a Torah precept of monumental consequence? Such seems to be the case regarding *kedoshim tihiyu,*[1] the commandment to become holy.

Kedoshim tihiyu is not ignored because of its obscurity. People readily understand what it is about. Part of it means avoiding all things that are the opposite of holy. Another component means moving toward something different: making the changes toward becoming a living essence of holiness. (The conclusion of the verse "because I am Hashem your God" alludes to this. You are to become holy like I am holy, meaning a holiness of essence, and not merely by avoiding the unholy.) Holiness is the source and foundation of the Jewish people and a critical part of its unique loftiness; it is its spiritual foundation.

The Zohar[2] takes note of the threefold use of the word "holy" in a single verse: "You are to sanctify yourselves and you shall be holy,

---

Based on *Netivot Shalom* 1:122–126.

1. Lev. 19:2.
2. Zohar 3:190.

for I am holy."[3] The Zohar sees in this an allusion to different forms of holiness in the worlds of *asiya, yetzira,* and *beria*.[4] These worlds mediate our actions, our spirit, and our souls. Practically, this means that we can find places for holiness in our deeds, in our wants and desires, and in bringing to light the bond between our souls and their source in the upper worlds.

If holiness is so basic and so important, why is its pursuit so neglected? The culprit seems to be a common and toxic misconception. Holiness is all about a lofty level of elevation, and many people see themselves – quite realistically – as so distant from this kind of attainment that any special quest for holiness appears remote and irrelevant.

This is a tragic error. *Kedoshim tihiyu* is a part of the Torah's script for us, just like all others. It applies to all Jews, regardless of their spiritual standing. It most certainly applies to Jews whose service of God is stuck in the world of *asiya,* the lowest level, still doing battle with themselves regarding activities that are completely forbidden. Were a person to argue that a particular mitzva of the Torah was not relevant to him, we would brand him a heretic. Why should we assume that *kedoshim tihiyu* is any different?

How is a person who is mired in his lowly desires supposed to approach the pursuit of holiness when he is so out of step with its nature? The answer is quite simple. The mitzva is in the attempt. A person must do whatever he can do. What he achieves thereafter is irrelevant. The fulfillment of the mitzva is in trying one's best.

The *Mesillat Yesharim*[5] explains the subtle difference between *tahara,* or purity, and *kedusha,* holiness. The former involves escaping from all contaminants. Because all material pursuits – even those entirely removed from any tinge of prohibition or impropriety – nudge a person closer to the material part of himself, the pure individual eschews any involvement with them, unless absolutely compelled to utilize them for his own survival.

---

3. Lev. 11:44.
4. Taken from the three verbs for "creating" at the beginning of Genesis, they are three of the four spiritual worlds referred to in much kabbalistic thought.
5. Ch. 26.

The holy individual, however, does not encourage one to run from things of this world, but warmly accepts them. The pure individual still needs to escape their appeal and their downward pull; the holy individual treasures each one as he elevates them, transforming their physicality into spirituality. The pure individual eats little so that the excess will not weigh him down; the holy individual turns his food into an offering. Both of them are part of the mitzva of *kedoshim tihiyu*, which the Ramban identifies with the epigram "sanctify yourself with what is permissible to you." This implies that a person will not be "a glutton with the permission of the Torah" – he will avoid excess. But it also indicates that he will take the objects that are permissible to him and sanctify them by elevating them.

The Torah exhorts us to holiness three times in *Parashat Kedoshim*, in reference to forbidden relations, idol worship, and forbidden foods. These references underscore three areas in which we need to strive for holiness. The connection to forbidden relations is obvious; Man easily loses his elevation and even his humanity in pursuing his lusts and desires in this area. The reference to idol worship instructs us to seek holiness in our system of beliefs. There are notions that we are not forbidden to harbor yet that diminish our pure and untarnished *emuna*, belief. Holiness implies keeping them at arm's length. The reference to food tells us to elevate the way we eat, even when our food products are kosher.

There are three distinct sources of holiness that are available to us from which to draw. Holiness resides in all our mitzvot and in the Torah we learn. (We make mention of this holiness in the blessing we recite: "*Asher kiddeshanu*," "Who has sanctified us.") Special times and seasons like Shabbat and the holidays are also fonts of special holiness available to us. (Here, too, we mention that holiness in the blessing that accompanies these times: "*Mekadesh Yisrael vehazemanim*," "Who sanctifies Yisrael and the festival seasons." This means that God sanctifies us by allowing us to draw holiness from the special appointed times.)

The third source is the most onerous. We find holiness in the hard work of breaking our lusts and desires. (The *Yesod HaAvoda* urged people to actively resist their wants and longings – even when no trace of sin was involved. We become masters of ourselves by resisting those inner voices that make demands upon us.) Our individual will is the fortress of the evil inclination, the place it can call home. Holiness, on the other hand, is the dominion of the soul from above. The will and the soul are locked in perpetual conflict for supremacy. When one rises, the other falls.

Curiously, the standard works that enumerate the 613 mitzvot fail to include "You shall be holy [*kedoshim tihiyu*]" (Lev. 19:2). Why is this all-important requirement not formally part of the inventory of divine demands upon us? We might find an answer to this question in the Ran's approach[6] to the *Akeda*, the Binding of Yitzhak. God begins His speech to Avraham, asking him to slaughter Yitzhak with the words *kah na*,[7] "take please." Our Sages[8] tell us that the word *na* has the effect of making this a request, not a demand. This means, says the Ran, that God never instructed Avraham to slaughter his son so much as revealed to him that He would be pleased if Avraham would do so. Avraham faced no divine retribution if he failed to comply. He acted completely volitionally, only to bring satisfaction, so to speak, to his Creator. The idea behind *kedoshim tihiyu* is the same. It differentiates between those who submit to the will of their Creator and those who love Him so much that they strive to please Him in everything they do. It is therefore in a class by itself and not cut of the same cloth as the 613 mitzvot.

In the final analysis, we are still plagued by a crucial question: If striving for holiness is relevant to all of us, how can its requirements be met by those of us who still find ourselves stuck in the clutches of the evil inclination, which does not let up and allows us no peace?

The Torah provides a model for us. We know that there are sections of the Torah ordered precisely as we would expect them to be. At the same time, we are aware of sections that are presented in the text out of the order in which they chronologically occurred.

The same holds true of our service of God. The active mitzvot allow for no change or innovation. They must be performed according to the specification of halakha, without deviation. Nothing else will do.

The mitzvot that apply to the inner person also follow a prescribed order. The requirements here, however, are not as exacting. At times,

---

6. *Derashot HaRan* 6.
7. Gen. 22:2.
8. Cited by Rashi, ibid.

a person can and should perform these mitzvot out of their assigned order. While we generally advocate desisting from evil before working on enhancing the good, there can be exceptions. A person must sometimes make progress by jumping over obstacles and – in what otherwise would be considered a premature step – reaching for a higher level. In *Ḥasidut*, this approach is called "over and over." When a person faces obstacles in his progress, when that progress in fighting the attraction of a sin proceeds too slowly, he must sometimes jump to a higher level of performance of the good.

How can this work? The explanation is quite simple. Sometimes, taking up residence on a higher plane gives a person the needed perspective to look down upon the evil within him, to detest it and thereby give him the resolve to do something about it.

The view is indeed different at the top, and we do not all arrive at the same place. Setting off on the journey, however, is expected of all of us.

You Shall Do What Is Right and Good

Y ou might expect that expert spiritual advice to practicing kabbalists would sound esoteric and otherworldly. We would not be surprised to find a recipe, for example, of one part meditation and two parts recombining the letters of God's holy names. Instead, The recommendations of the *Shomer Emunim*[1] are so down to earth that even non-kabbalist will cheer.

Don't let go of two verses, he writes. Keep them forever on your lips. "*Ve'asita hayashar vehatov*," "And you shall do what is right and good in the eyes of Hashem,"[2] is one of them. The other is "*Kedoshim tihiyu*," "You shall be holy."[3] These two commandments are special because they include many mitzvot and prohibitions that are not explicitly mentioned in the Torah.

Based on *Netivot Shalom* 1:137–139.
1. Introduction, sections 2–3.
2. Deut. 6:18.
3. Lev. 19:2.

The Ramban takes note of the fact that our Sages understand *ve'asita hayashar vehatov* as instruction to go beyond the requirements of the law. First, he tells us, the Torah commands us to scrupulously observe the commandments that it specifically commands. Then, he says, it turns to areas that are not legislated and asks us to be sure to do what is right and good, since this is, after all, what God holds dear.

This instruction is crucial, because it covers what otherwise would be a huge gap in the law. The Torah legislates liberally regarding interpersonal relations. But it is impossible to be comprehensive through fixed laws and statutes. So much depends on circumstances and the personalities of the individuals involved. The Torah essentially tells us to legislate for ourselves – to extend the ethic of goodness that we find running through the other mitzvot and apply it as it fits each unique situation that arises.

The Ramban's treatment of *kedoshim tihiyu* is remarkably similar. Here, too, specific statutes regarding intimacy and food spell out what the Torah prohibits and what it permits. But these laws are not sufficiently comprehensive to produce people about whom God can be proud. They leave ample room for missing the overarching ethos of the mitzva system. A person can keep well within those laws and still remain a "glutton within the law." *Kedoshim tihiyu* demands that we police ourselves, insuring that we fly high above the storm clouds of physical excess.

Our Sages had their own names for each of the five books of the Torah. Curiously, they [4] called Genesis *Sefer HaYashar*, the book of the upright. We would have expected that Genesis's name would reflect some aspect of "beginning" – Creation, birth of humanity, or birth of the Jewish people. Perhaps our Sages focused on something even more important. As we said above, many have asked why the Torah does not explicitly prohibit bad character traits, especially since banishing them is of such high priority. The answer may be that it does, that this is precisely the function of Genesis!

Genesis can be seen as a law book, as legislating not by statute but by example. The narratives in the early part of the Bible demonstrate the pitfalls of bad character traits. Kayin's downfall came through jealousy.

---

4. Avoda Zara 25a.

The generation of the flood needed to be wiped off the face of the earth because it had capitulated to lust and desire. The builders of the Tower of Babel allowed the pursuit of honor to run away with itself and with their very lives.[5] The story of Sodom shows us the consequences of cruelty; we learn to recoil from bad character through the stories of Esav, Lavan, and Shekhem.

We also learn in Genesis how good should supplant the evil we avoid. This is the overarching theme of the lives of our forefathers. We see them begin the long process of *tikkun*, with Avraham instructing us about *ḥesed*, and Yitzḥak and Yaakov demonstrating *gevura*, a *midda* related to strength or restraint, and *tiferet*, a combination of *ḥesed* and *gevura*. Yosef teaches us about *yesod*, the positive *midda* that incorporates all the others.

All of this – the rejection of evil and the embrace of proper character traits under the banner of constantly pursuing what is right and good – set the stage for our receiving the Torah at Sinai. God reached out to us with much hand-holding to get us there. At the time of the Exodus, we were not paragons of virtuous conduct. We were not theologically sophisticated either. Seven weeks of intense, programmed experience readied us for that great moment at the foot of the mountain.

We did meet one requirement, however. We were expected to first arrive at a point at which we could properly be called Jewish. We succeeded at this, but only because we took the path charted by our forefathers. No other path could have gotten us there. Genesis, therefore, can be seen as the story of preparing the way for the receiving of the Torah that follows in Exodus. Calling Genesis *Sefer HaYashar* makes eminent sense. It sums up the mission of the forefathers – transmitting the essential qualities of Jewishness to their descendants.

Every Jew individually must travel the same route. Our Jewishness is conferred upon us if we are born to the right parents. We have no say in this, nor do we earn it. On the other hand, if we wish to view ourselves as essentially Jewish by dint of our own activity, there is no

---

5. For a fuller development of this theme, see Yitzchok Adlerstein, *Nesivos Shalom: Thoughts on the Weekly Parsha*, vol. 1 (2012), "Bereishis: Roadmap to Kabbolas HaTorah," 3–8.

way other than to take on the attributes and the pursuit of the right and good that characterized our forefathers.

Further scrutinizing the phrase "right and good," we realize that the Torah speaks of two very different pursuits. *Yashar*, right, refers to our relationship with others and with God Himself. "Good" in our context refers to holiness. (We noted above that holiness is linked to *yesod*. Shortcomings in the *midda* of *yesod*[6] are often referred to simply as "bad." It follows that the perfection of this trait should be called "good.")

We now understand why the list of 613 mitzvot does not include these signposts of Jewish living that we have discussed here. These pursuits define the mission and purpose of Jewish living; they make us fully Jewish. Jews are commanded to perform mitzvot, but there is no mitzva to become a Jew. *Ve'asita hayashar vehatov* is the slogan that instructs us how to get there.

---

6. "Shortcomings in *yesod*" is a frequent euphemism for sexual wrongdoing.

Elul

The World of Repentance

Teshuva, repentance, is not an exit strategy for the sinner. It is not a process or a procedure. Repentance reaches so far and so deep that we must view it as a parallel universe.

Repentance is a vital element in the life of a Jew. It is part and parcel of his very Jewishness. Repentance applies to everyone – not just to the evildoer but to the average person and even to a righteous individual, on a lofty plane. Similarly, it applies at all times in a person's life. It applies when a person reaches a nadir in his spirituality, when his spiritual existence is clouded and dark, as well as at times of heightened spiritual elevation.

The Sages created a standard formula for prayer for all Jews without exception. In the *Shemoneh Esreh*, every Jew turns to the Almighty morning, afternoon, and night with important requests that cover our spiritual and material needs. After asking for understanding and comprehension we continue, "Bring us back to Your Torah, bring us close to Your service, and return us to complete repentance before You." Repentance clearly is on the short list of the most essential spiritual needs of all Jews.

Based on *Netivot Shalom* 1:195–198.

All this enlightens us regarding the position and role of repentance. If repentance's importance is universal, then we must think of it not merely as a contrivance for dealing with human failure. It is at once the most basic of all levels – an outgrowth of the supernal will that no person ever be pushed away – as well as the highest of levels, suitable to the needs of the absolutely righteous. "There is none in the land who is righteous, who does good and does not sin."[1] No matter how great the *tzaddik*, he does not reach the pinnacle of perfection. He may understand much about the greatness of God and act accordingly in avoiding evil and performing good deeds. Nonetheless, anyone standing before the King of kings, whose unlimited greatness is unknowable to mortal flesh and blood, must possess some defect owing to a lack of appreciation of the true loftiness of *Ein Sof*, the Infinite One. Accordingly, God created repentance, allowing us to compensate for all imperfection. Thus, the righteous one, who has no sin for which to repent, employs the world of repentance to burnish his good deeds, using its power to add luster to them.

Repentance, then, is the vehicle to complete and perfect the life of every Jew. Our Sages[2] see repentance as one of a few elements that God put into place even before Creation. Repentance was a necessary precursor of existence, even before man was created, or tasted of sin. Without repentance, the world simply cannot get to its goal of a perfected society.

We will thus not make the common error of viewing repentance as a form of expiating sin – a protocol to secure forgiveness for misdeeds, to express remorse, and restore the relationship to where it stood before the sin. So many passages in classic rabbinic texts do not allow such a reading but support the idea that repentance is something new and something substantive. It is new in the sense of not setting the clock back to where it was earlier but creating something more elegant than that which it replaces. Thus, our Sages tell us[3] that repentance brings healing to the entire world, and it brings redemption to the entire world. "In the

---

1. Eccl. 7:20.
2. Pesaḥim 54a.
3. Yoma 86b.

place of those who have repented, the complete *tzaddik* cannot stand."[4]
The Rambam's words[5] are particularly instructive: "Great is repentance,
which brings a person close to the Divine Presence…. Whereas a person was previously detested and distant from God, he now is beloved
and cherished." Repentance is seen as taking the repentant sinner to a
place greater than where he was before he sinned at all.

We can explain the wider curative effect of repentance by way
of analogy to a king whose treasury was plundered in a brazen attack
on the royal palace. One of the king's subjects risks his life to penetrate
the enemy camp and singlehandedly liberates the stolen treasure. The
operation demonstrates so much dedication on the part of this brave
subject and brings so much honor to the king that he showers benefits
upon the entire realm.

In truth, the dedication of one who has repented is but one element that makes repentance so potent. Another element is the magic
that repentance works on its practitioner. As our Sages point out,[6]
human reason would predict that there is no way to evade the strict
consequences of any sin. Transgressions are not arbitrary; each one represents something harmful to us. When we damage one of our limbs or
organs, we become less functional. The body does not replenish a lost
limb or organ. Why should our spiritual selves work any differently?
Repentance, however, does more than reconcile humans and their
Divine Father. Repentance does not slap a new coat of paint on an old
structure. Repentance builds anew from the ground up. One who has
repented is given not an extension of his life but a new life. He is not the
person he was previously. (This is perhaps the most incisive explanation
of why the righteous person cannot stand in the same place as one who
has repented. Because "there is none in the land who is righteous… and
does not sin," it follows that the righteous person is not entirely free of
any blemish. One who has repented, on the other hand, stands blessed
with the innocence of a newborn.) The Rambam's advice[7] to those who

---

4. Berakhot 34b.
5. *Hilkhot Teshuva* 7:6.
6. Y. Makkot 2:6.
7. *Hilkhot Teshuva* 2:4.

have repented also flows from this reality. "Among the ways of repentance is that the person changes his name, as if to say, 'I am another! I am not the one who sinned and acted in that way.'" Repentance connotes a complete change of being.

Even the conventional form of repentance – regret for one's conduct – includes more than we generally realize. We must examine not only our actions but our inner selves as well. We will then find ourselves repenting not only for misconduct but for our personality flaws and bad traits. We will find ourselves lacking in spiritual outlook and attitude – sometimes harboring ideas that border on the heretical.

Some of us will face a tougher challenge when we realize that we need to repudiate our entire lifestyle. We might be relatively free of sin and yet realize that our lives have become so mired in the pursuit of the material that we are preoccupied with unworthy goals. We will then require a much broader kind of repentance.

A still more difficult challenge awaits a person whose lifestyle has become empty of any spiritual content. He possesses no spiritual longing, has no spiritual vision, and feels no stirrings of holiness even on the special days of Shabbat and the holidays. His repentance will need to be even more intense.

The most daunting repentance challenge is posed to the person who is clueless about its very need. He feels nothing wrong and has no inclination to do repentance, nor has he any inkling that he needs to. Repentance for such a person will be difficult, indeed.

The difficulty, however, is no match for the power of repentance to turn a person into a new being. Such power can overcome all difficulties. It is available for the asking.

Complete Repentance

The blessing in the *Shemoneh Esreh* that deals with repentance speaks of our returning to God "in complete repentance." We ask for many things in our fixed prayer, but we don't make completeness an integral part of the request. We may go for broke, but in many gifts we are content to take what we can get. What is it about repentance that makes us a bit pushier in what we request? Wouldn't asking God to help us do repentance be sufficient – without specifying quantity or quality?

Something unique to repentance, apparently, demands that it be complete. If it is not, it will come up short.

It might very well be that complete repentance is important to us because we are so familiar with the other kind. Regret can come easily to many a person. He can cry his heart out before God, and yet his repentance will predictably be brief and fleeting if he lacks the prerequisites for effectiveness. When we ask for complete repentance, we may not be talking about the quality and depth of the repentance so much as requesting that we are able to come to the repentance table with the understanding and attitudes necessary to make it work. Without some

---

Based on *Netivot Shalom* 1:207–209.

conceptual tools working for us, our repentance will be incomplete – and necessarily brief.

The most important of those precursors is full understanding of the seriousness of sin. Complete repentance requires understanding of the framework and context of transgression. The evil inclination typically tells us that our sin is a small thing. It does not allow us to contemplate its implications, including the wedge that sin drives between ourselves and our heavenly Father, and the darkness that envelops all of the spiritual worlds as its consequence. If we do not stop to think about how sin harms us and the world, our repentance will be superficial.

A person who is oblivious to the reality of the horror of sin dwells in utter confusion. Kabbalistic literature speaks of a state worse than Gehenna. Some people wander through life, oblivious to the requirements of law. They sin without any awareness of its weightiness. They experience no divine retribution for decades. When they die, they are treated similarly. Even Gehenna is inappropriate for them. They continue to wander without judgment or accounting in what is called *olam hatohu*, an existence of astonishing chaos. To a certain extent, the *olam hatohu* spills over into our world, experienced by people still alive. These people glide in and out of the Days of Awe, oblivious to their sanctity and meaning, as if unsure in which world they reside.

Such people cannot do repentance properly. If they are stirred somehow to repent, their turnaround will not last. For this reason, when we ask God's help in doing repentance in *Shemoneh Esreh*, we first request that He return us to His Torah, and bring us closer to His service. Torah and service of God open our eyes to the true, deadly nature of sin. Only then can we hope to achieve what we next ask of Him: complete repentance, repentance with our eyes open to the meaning of sin.

Another possible meaning of "complete repentance" emerges from the words of the Rambam.[1] He tells us that the fullness of repentance requires that we find ourselves faced with comparable circumstances and temptation as when we first sinned. In the comparable situation, however, we avoid the snare of sin. One who sinned with a particular woman fully repents only when he is once again alone with

---

1. *Hilkhot Teshuva* 2:1.

her, his desire for her unabated, his strength intact – but this time he manages to overcome his evil inclination. If he repents only when he is much older, his repentance is not full, but is nonetheless effective, at least to some extent. Even when done on his deathbed, his repentance serves to gain for him forgiveness for his sin – but the complete repentance that we seek accomplishes far more than mere forgiveness.

The *Yesod HaAvoda* explains that complete repentance must come from the depths of one's heart, preparing one to withstand future temptation. This kind of repentance indeed uproots sin from its source retroactively.

We can draw a parallel from the laws of *kashering* utensils. The overarching rule is one of equivalent effect: that the non-kosher substance absorbed in the walls of a pot can be drawn out the same way it entered in the first place. (If, for example, non-kosher flavor was absorbed in the presence of direct heat, the pot can be purged of that flavor only by the application of direct heat.) Similarly, we commit sins with varying amounts of passion. When we sin with great passion, our repentance is not complete until we can resist in the presence of great passion. It takes great internal resolve to resist that great passion; that resolve is what undoes the sin. Complete repentance, then, would include the opportunity to feel remorse equal in intensity to the sin we committed.

Another explanation of complete repentance is that it be appropriate to its milieu. In fighting a military battle, it is important to know what material the other side will bring to the front. If they come equipped with heavy armaments, you will lose the battle before even beginning if all you can muster is small arms. Similarly, it is important to inventory what the evil inclination brings to the front. In earlier times, the *Sitra Aḥra* (literally, "the other side," a reference to the forces of evil) did not manifest itself as brazenly and openly as it does today. Today, the air itself is thick with impurity, corruption, and heresy. These have penetrated the gates of Jerusalem itself, reaching even to the holiest sites. What used to get by as repentance is inadequate at the moment. Today's penitent must take into account the realities of the next assault by the evil inclination. At the same time, a Jew must keep in mind that balance is designed into the system. As the powers of evil seem to grow, we can be sure that God makes available to us parallel powers of holiness to offset them.

Complete repentance might also mean a repentance that encompasses the entire person. When repentance occurs through the mind alone or through feeling alone, it is in danger of eventually failing. The most effective repentance will address the head, insuring that outlooks and attitudes are faithful to God's expectations. It will work on the heart, changing its wants and feelings into holiness. It will alter the character traits that manifest themselves as activity of the limbs. As repentance envelops the entirety of a person, the words of Psalms[2] accurately describe him: "All my limbs will say 'Hashem, who is like you?'" He becomes a personification of "My heart and my flesh shout joyfully to the living God."[3]

As was the case with the other explanations of complete repentance that we offered above, it is the comprehensiveness of the repentance that assures its longevity. The very possibility of repentance manifests the extraordinary *ḥesed* of God toward us. It accomplishes so much, given the stakes involved, and the forces that are arrayed to oppose it and to erode it even when we have succeeded in doing it. If we are aware of this, we should be in a better position to reinforce it by making it indeed a "complete repentance."

---

2. Ps. 35:10.
3. Ibid. 84:3.

The Context of Evildoing

Context means everything. Focusing narrowly on our deeds, misdeeds, and even repentance itself without understanding their greater context will yield only minor gains for us relative to much effort. We need to understand the larger picture, the backdrop against which proper and improper actions are set and into which the Holy One, blessed be He, set the all-important opportunity of repentance.

The value of context is the inescapable conclusion from Isaiah's famous exhortation "Let the wicked one forsake his way and the iniquitous man his thoughts."[1] What makes the sinner wicked if not his actions and deeds? What should the sinner be asked to forsake if not his evil actions? Why speak about some nebulous "way" rather than his concrete failings? Isaiah tells us that it is even more important for the sinner to look at his "way" in sin than looking at the sins themselves.

The road back for the sinner begins with his abandoning that way – the pattern that led him repeatedly to do evil. Similarly, he must give up the thoughts – the modes of thinking and outlooks – from which

---

Based on *Netivot Shalom* 1:209–212.

1. Is. 55:2.

his transgression sprang. This is consistent with a theme of kabbalistic literature, that the evil inclination need not lure a person anew for each sin, but simply move a person to its territory and turf, an entire world that is a "place" of easy sin.

What is the context of evildoing, this place of easy wrongdoing? "See, I have placed before you today the life and the good and the death and the evil.... And you shall choose life so that you and your offspring shall live."[2] Why do we need to be prodded toward life? Once we can recognize the difference between life and death, do we still need to be urged to choose it?

Indeed we must. Since God wills it that we be given the opportunity to exercise free will, we must always have competing alternatives. Humans generally find purposeful building satisfying. We enjoy creating. We accept these facts as hardwired in the human spirit. We should not be surprised, however, to discover other tendencies, ones that are darker and more sinister. We observe that humans take pleasure not only in building and creating, but in tearing down and destroying. The evil inclination can influence a person to enjoy foods, lifestyles, and attitudes that are self-destructive (like anger and revenge) or destructive of others.

We watch curiously as toddlers seem to delight in breaking things and we do not realize that adults are not so different. They, too, enjoy causing havoc and chaos. This carries over to the community as well. We observe nations perennially dedicating resources to the destruction of other nations, investing enormous energy into the development of greater destructive capacity against the other. Destructiveness has become, as it were, a vital force within human civilization.

Character flaws also populate this background of evildoing. The Rambam writes,[3] "Do not say that repentance applies only to sins involving action. Just as a person must repent of those, he must also examine his evil traits and repent of anger and hatred and jealously and frivolousness and the pursuit of money and honor and gluttony." This is also implied in the phrase "Let the wicked one forsake

---

2. Deut. 30:15, 19.
3. *Hilkhot Teshuva* 7:3.

his way." So long as a person has not addressed his character flaws, he is in the thrall of the evil inclination even when he does nothing actively wrong.

The *Yesod HaAvoda* offers an example of a king who seeks to prepare his son for eventual rule and wishes to promote in him the best inner qualities. While the prince is in the company of his father, the son's inner core cannot be discerned. The king's presence is palpable; his influence irresistible. The king sends the prince to a distant part of the realm. There, where the king's authority is present but not overt, the prince is at first drawn to act like the coarse people around him. In time, however, he becomes dissatisfied with these leanings and recognizes the weaknesses in his character that made him vulnerable to them. Realizing that the day approaches when he will be reunited with his father, the prince prepares for the encounter. He understands that he can best prepare for his future relationship with the king by addressing his inner self. The better the job he does, the more satisfying the relationship will be. The *Yesod HaAvoda* likens the descent of the soul to this world to the prince sent from the presence of the father. Taking note of our own leanings and predilections in response to the world around us allows us to more realistically appraise ourselves and the work we need to do to refine our character.

Another component of the landscape of evildoing is tunnel vision regarding the majesty of creation. Animals walk on all fours. Their long axis runs parallel to the ground; their eyes are often fixed on the ground in front of them. Their world, therefore, is the feeding trough. Man, however, walks erect. He lifts up his head and sees afar. He can see God within the fullness of His creation.

Some people do not escape their animal selves. They, too, live a limited existence. Grown people find it amusing when they watch a young child's attachment to a worthless plaything. If that toy is taken away from the child, he wails as if his world had come to an end. But are adults so different? With what do they preoccupy themselves? What makes them happy? About what do they fritter away valuable time worrying? Are any of those things comparable to the Torah and mitzvot, which could gain them eternity? Are adults different from children, or have they merely replaced one kind of toy with another?

Our Sages had this in mind when they wrote,[4] "A person does not sin unless a spirit of lunacy enters into him." This lunacy is a worldview in which the trivial and unimportant become his objects of pursuit. The Saba Kadisha used to say that in every sin, the spirit of lunacy and folly accounts for 99 percent of his decision; concession to the evil inclination amounts to only the remaining 1 percent.

When a person lives with constricted understanding, everything surrounding him is limited and shriveled. His Torah is narrow; it fails to fill the depth and breadth of halakha. His service of God is constricted; he fails to "taste and see that God is good."[5]

There is a context and backdrop to repentance as well. Its most important element is the longing of the holy spark within each person – the "portion of God from Above" – for its root and source. The Jewish soul always thirsts for more, each person according to his spiritual level. Only the person whose multiple sins have done severe damage to his personality can be stripped of the emotional longing of the typical Jew. This thirst is what neutralizes the destruction-bent forces within the evil inclination.

Making use of this repentance context follows a distinct pattern. The *Tur* begins the *Shulḥan Arukh* by reminding us how transgressions are committed: "The eye sees, the heart desires, and the limbs complete the action." Repentance works similarly. First, a person must turn his eyes upward and behold the One who has created everything. He then arouses his heart and thirsts for connection with Divinity. His limbs then allow him to right his course and actualize his repentance through action.

Part of the context of repentance is listening. When the Torah describes national repentance, it writes,[6] "And you will return to Hashem your God and listen to His voice." We would have expected the Torah to write, "And you will do all that I have commanded you." Instead, the Torah instructs us regarding the first step in repentance, after we have moved to a repentance context. We first must listen to the sound of

---

4. Sota 3a.
5. Ps. 34:9.
6. Deut. 30:2.

God knocking[7] on the walls of our hearts. We must realize, as the Baal Shem Tov taught, that the heavenly voice which calls us each day to repentance[8] may not be heard physically by us but is heard and heeded by our *neshamot*.

In the final analysis, repentance does require that we take action. Placing our inner selves within the context of repentance, inspiring ourselves spiritually and intellectually, and taking pains to hear the voices bidding us to return – all these are insufficient. They cannot make us repent without concomitant action.

This action also needs to be placed within the context of our individual needs and requirements. We need to turn the inspiration into individually tailored actions, addressing our core flaws and problems. The *Beit Yosef*, for example, first addressed stiff-neckedness by realizing the importance of bending his will to that of the Creator. He then translated that realization through an individual action plan: he loaded rocks upon his shoulders to physically cause him to bend. This is a perfect example of giving substance to an inner realization by coupling it with action. Another effective method is to simply increase the number of the good things we are already doing. As the midrash says,[9] "If a person was accustomed to learning one page of Torah, he should begin to learn two."

The bottom line is that we will best succeed if we take a broader view of our assets, our flaws, and the tools that are the most effective – as well as embrace the deep desire within us to feel the presence of God.

---

7. An allusion to Song. 5:2.
8. Zohar 3:126a.
9. Leviticus Rabba 25:1.

The Days of Awe

The Trembling of the Angels

Hug your judge" is not a slogan that has gone viral.

Judges are not the first individuals we associate with warmth, affection, and closeness. Rosh HaShana requires us to relate to God as Judge,[1] more so than any other time of the year. This makes perfect sense on the day that the entire world is judged, and the future of all hangs in the balance. At the same time, our Sages[2] speak of the Ten Days of Repentance as the time that He is closest and most accessible. How is this compatible with focusing on God as Judge?

However we envision the God as Judge in our mind's eye, the Torah itself makes no mention of His being the Judge on this all-important day. Instead, this day is somewhat elliptically described as a "remembrance of the *terua*."

Based on *Netivot Shalom* 2:107–112.

1. The passage from the Zohar recited before the sounding of the shofar stresses God's love for justice and the need to remind the world that there is judgment as well as a Judge.
2. Rosh HaShana 18a.

Rosh HaShana is rife with contradictory moods and mixed metaphors. What demeanor is appropriate on a day of such awesome consequence? With our lives hanging in the balance, we would expect to be somber, brooding, and dejected about the sorry state of our spiritual portfolios. Unlike on other holidays, we refrain from reciting Hallel. How could we, asks the Gemara,[3] when the books of life and death are open before the Judge? Yet, we are instructed to treat it as a holiday. Psalms[4] refers to it as a *ḥag*, a celebratory holiday. We laud it in our praying as a day given to us by God with love.

Rosh HaShana's established role as the day of divine accounting and judgment disappears precisely where you would expect it to show itself. In our praying, we do not (unlike Yom Kippur) look back at our behavior of the previous year. We do not stand in contrition and remorse (again, unlike Yom Kippur), offering tearful pleas for forgiveness. Most importantly, throughout the long and beautiful Rosh HaShana prayers, this all-too-obvious theme of divine judgment is given only passing mention by an oblique reference here and there. Why do we not put this idea front and center?

Even the judgment aspects of Rosh HaShana puzzle us. Who has not been moved by the haunting words of the *Unetaneh Tokef* prayer, with its chilling evocation of the awesomeness of divine judgment? According to it, even the angels tremble!

Angels? Trembling? Whatever for? Do angels have free will? Do they get it wrong, like we do? Is there a book of life for angels?

The mystery starts with Torah itself. The Torah points to the themes of the different holidays: freedom on Passover, joy on Sukkot, atonement and purification on Yom Kippur. A few are left out. Why isn't the Torah more up-front about Shavuot being the time of our receiving of the Torah at Sinai? Our Sages tell us what Shemini Atzeret is about, but why is the text of the Torah virtually silent about its theme? As mentioned above, the Torah describes Rosh HaShana only with an

---

3. Ibid. 32b.
4. Ps. 81:4.

oblique reference to the sounding of the shofar. It tells us what we do on the day, but not what the day is.

If we look for the essence of Rosh HaShana in the judgment theme, we are looking in the wrong place. Judgment is the consequence, not the core idea.

Rosh HaShana marks the annual renewal of the world. It is the anniversary of the creation of man, the purpose and culmination of all of creation. On this day, explains the Ari, all things return to their prehistory. The world is licensed one year at a time. At the end of a yearly period, it must be created anew.

Shabbat has a similar function. The *Or HaHayim*[5] teaches us that God places just enough of whatever it takes for the world to last for six days. Existence passes to the next week only through what He invests in it each Shabbat.

The Ari taught that Rosh HaShana works similarly. The unit of time that we call a year has real substance in the eyes of God. When it comes to an end, all things return to where they came from. They are put back into effect, into what we experience as existence, only through the vehicle of Rosh HaShana.

This is the true central theme of Rosh HaShana, a theme so profound that the Torah did not wish to confine it to words – just as it does not explicitly describe the role of other days of the greatest holiness, like Shavuot and Shemini Atzeret. (Those days as well contain elements of unusual holiness that cannot be limited by human speech.)[6] All other aspects of Rosh HaShana flow directly from this theme and are subservient to it.

The annual renewal begins with an accounting of all things. It measures the performance of each and every element of the world, measuring how it fits into God's grand scheme for the unfolding of human history. Elements that are not performing, or are no longer needed, simply disappear into the abyss of the past. They are not recreated. The

---

5. *Or HaHayim* on Gen. 2:3.
6. They both represent holiness beyond its usual manifestation, which is symbolized by the number seven, like the Sabbath day. Shavuot is on the fiftieth day, or the one after seven times seven; Shemini Atzeret is the eighth day.

world's lease on life expires; a new one is granted only to those receiving passing marks in the annual checkup.

This has nothing to do with free will. It applies to absolutely everyone and everything, Jew and non-Jew, animate and inanimate. It even applies to the angels.

As powerful a concept as this is, it is only half the picture. Our tradition tells us that whatever it is that this world is supposed to accomplish, the Jewish people are the vehicles to make it happen. The equation becomes frighteningly simple. No Jewish people, God forbid, no world. If there is a renewal of the world each Rosh HaShana, it follows that there is a necessary and parallel renewal and reinvention of the covenant between God and us. "You all stand this day before Hashem… that you should be entered into a covenant with Hashem your God."[7] The plain meaning of the text refers to the words of reproach and encouragement that Moshe gave to the Jews in the wilderness at the end of his life. Kabbalistic works see an allusion in the words "this day" to a continuing event: to Rosh HaShana each year and our standing before God in a new covenant. The ability of the Jewish people to implement God's design, to carry His wishes closer to completion, is the essence of "crowning" Him as the regnant power on earth. Each year on Rosh HaShana, we renew His coronation by renewing the covenant between us.

This covenant is the reestablishment not only of the fact of the relationship between us, but of the quality of that relationship. Without one special quality, we simply cannot do our job. This all-important quality is the breaking of all barriers between a Jew and his heavenly Father. There are, ultimately, no veils, no curtains, no walls between the heart and soul of a Jew who seeks closeness with his Creator.

The Gemara[8] illustrates the point by contrasting two kinds of connection. Many Jews fell to the wiles of the Midianite women and became attached, *nitzmadim*,[9] to Baal-Peor. Not long afterward the survivors are praised by Moshe as also being attached – properly so, this time – to God. The word that the Torah uses there, however, is not *nitzmadim*

---

7. Deut. 29:9, 11.
8. Sanhedrin 64a.
9. Num. 25:3.

but *devekim*. The Gemara sees common ground in the word *nitzmadim* and *tzamid*, a woman's bracelet. Rashi explains: A bracelet is attached but free to move in place, from side to side. *Devekut*, clinging, connotes a yet stronger attachment.

We've been there before. At Mount Sinai, we attached ourselves to Him so perfectly that our souls fled our bodies. This is part of what Rabbenu Saadia Gaon meant when he included Sinai as one of the ten items we are reminded of through the sounding of the shofar on Rosh HaShana. Each year, some spark of the *devekut* we felt at Sinai is available to us on Rosh HaShana, as we renew the covenant between God and ourselves. It, too, as well as the divine judgment, is an outgrowth of the main theme of Rosh HaShana: the renewal of the world, and the renewal of the special relationship between God and His people. Part of this renewal is providing us with the spiritual wherewithal to continue serving Him adequately. Thus, at least for those who understand and accept the mission, it is a time of forgiveness. Without that forgiveness, we are spiritually lamed and cannot fulfill our purpose.

The sense of *devekut* does not dissipate after Rosh HaShana. It grows, reaching a climax on Yom Kippur. On that day, at the time of most intense connection, it is the attachment to God itself that eradicates our sins. Since all sin is imperfection, no sin can exist within God. Thus, when we are united with God, our sins are left with no place to go.

There is no contradiction between seeing God as Judge and feeling confident in His forgiveness. If we pass muster in the key area of our commitment to His service, the details of our past mistakes can be dealt with without trauma.

This event is cause enough to treat Rosh HaShana as a holiday. This is why the *maḥzor*, the holiday prayer book, returns again and again to the theme of proclaiming God's kingship and slips in only a few mostly oblique references to the strictness of His judgment. Our job on Rosh HaShana is to recommit ourselves to the mission of His service. The rest is commentary.

Not so easy, you say? The explanation is elegant and compelling, but can we meaningfully access this possibility of *devekut*? Do we really get there?

Listen to the advice of the Zohar.[10] In gratitude for her hospitality, Elisha asked the Shunamite woman, "What can be done for you? Would you like to speak to the king or to the general?" She demurred. I don't really have any issues with people in high places like them, she explained. "I dwell among my people." The Zohar tells us that this dialogue occurred on Rosh HaShana, and addressed what weighs on most people's minds.

"Today is the day of judgment," said Elisha. "Would you like me to take up your case with God? I can try to put in a good word."

"Thanks, but not really," she answered. "I will take my chances from within the Jewish people as a whole. I do not wish to be singled out."

She was correct, says the Zohar. Our best position is to situate ourselves well within the Jewish people. God's compassion toward *Klal Yisrael* in its entirety never wavers.

After each round of shofar sounding we ask God's compassion, "either as children or as servants." This is really what Rosh HaShana is all about. Will we be judged to be mere servants, or will God see us as His children, as united and connected as family members?

The practical consequence of this passage from the Zohar is clear. Closeness to God is within range on Rosh HaShana. If we do not feel it innately, we ought to accentuate the parts of our service of God that require the many, rather than the individual in the privacy of his own thoughts and deeds. We need to pitch in with the community, to serve God as a part of the larger group. In this way, we open ourselves up to the embrace of the heavenly Father. As we feel that closeness, we can sign on to the new covenant that is formalized on that day, and in the process, sign ourselves into the book of life.

---

10. Zohar 2:44b.

Devekut Done Twice

Nehemya's advice to a chastened nation seems strange. "Today is holy to Hashem.... Go, eat rich foods and drink sweet drinks. Send portions to those who have nothing prepared.... Do not be sad. The enjoyment of Hashem is your strength!"[1] Nehemya's audience, no paragons of virtue, had good reason to cry any day of the year. They had many misdeeds that they needed to acknowledge. All the more so on Rosh HaShana, when they accepted their guilt and understood that they were standing before God who was judging them at that moment. We would think that crying would have been both cathartic and beneficial to their repentance.

Moreover, the Ari measured the sensitivity of our souls by our ability to cry. He looked down upon any person who could pass through the Days of Awe without shedding a tear. Why would Nehemya suppress the tears of his people and even urge them to eat celebratory meals?

The Yerushalmi[2] turns Nehemya's speech into policy for all time. "Ordinarily, a person awaiting judgment sits as if in mourning. Yisrael

Based on *Netivot Shalom* 2:113–115.

1. Neh. 8:9–10.
2. Y. Rosh HaShana 1:3.

does not do that. They dress in finery, eat, and drink, secure in the knowledge that God will perform the miraculous for them." Is not Rosh HaShana supposed to be a time of awe, in which we see ourselves submitting to the judgment of Heaven? How can we expect a miracle when we understand how vulnerable we are because of our sins?

The *Torat Avot* teaches that all of our repentance and self-improvement should take place not on Rosh HaShana, but prior to it, during the month of Elul. Repentance is not the theme of Rosh HaShana. That day is reserved for the coronation of the King, for accepting His authority over every part of our being. While the word *shana* means "year" in our world, it means something quite different in the upper worlds, in which there is no time. There, the word is related to *shinui*, "change." The new "year" in that world means the capacity to effect newness and change in the inhabitants of our world.

Our job on Rosh HaShana is to take advantage of that capacity for change. There is only one known way for that to happen on short notice – the promotion of *devekut*, firm connection with and clinging to God. By firmly accepting His kingship we can enter into a new relationship, a new covenant with Him. Casting away the old baggage, we meaningfully connect to Him.

Where there is a relationship of *devekut*, there is no room for judgment to take its toll upon us. *Din* cannot coexist with *devekut*. Indeed, we can celebrate in anticipation of a miraculous turnaround, at least in our relationship with God.

We stand at the threshold of understanding the enigmatic nature of a year's beginning that lasts not one day, but two. Can two be one? Apparently so, according to kabbalistic works. Halakha treats the two days of Rosh HaShana as one long day.[3] Standing at the core of this matter is the kernel of truth that the two days are treated similarly but are sourced in two entirely different ways of relating to God. The two days allow for us to revisit both *ahava* and *yira*, love and fear. Jointly, the two produce *devekut*.

Love and fear are two all-important pillars of our relationship with God. They tug at our heartstrings in very different ways. Mentally

---

3. Beitza 30b.

and emotionally, they draw out different responses from us. We shift inner gears between them, as they seem to address different aspects of ourselves. Between the two days of Rosh HaShana, the aspects of love and fear must each in a brief period of time arrive at the same place – namely, a rejuvenated, fierce sense of connection between the Jewish people and their Creator.

Love intuitively leads to *devekut*. Fear, however important, would not seem to get to the same place. When fear and overwhelming awe enter a relationship, we tend to flee in fright, or at least draw back. We certainly do not move closer. How can awe lead to *devekut*?

The *Peri Haaretz*[4] explains. The fear arises in part from the realization of God as the complete and absolute Giver, and ourselves as complete receivers. Focusing further upon this, we realize that we do not merely owe myriad blessings and favors to God; we owe Him everything. Understanding our complete dependence upon Him, we can more readily give up our sense of self to Him and arrive at a place of complete *bittul*, self-negation. Yielding to Him, removing the self-made barriers between ourselves and Him, allows for *devekut*.

The centrality of *devekut* on Rosh HaShana manifests itself in several other ways as well. We can easily see it peeking out in the three books in which we are all inscribed. The righteous individual merits immediate inscription in the book of life, while the *beinoni*, the person who falls between the righteous individual and the evildoer, navigates the Ten Days of Repentance before he is inscribed. Both must attain some level of *devekut* to renew the relationship with God for another year. The righteous one accomplishes this on Rosh HaShana and need wait no longer to be inscribed for life. The *beinoni* takes longer. He requires the Ten Days of Repentance to get him there, and therefore must wait till Yom Kippur to be inscribed.

The sounding of the shofar as well is shaped by the need to get to *devekut*. In times of war, we sound the broken blasts of the *terua* on the *hatzotzrot*, trumpets, which function to rouse the camp in the face of impending danger.[5] The sound is therefore associated with fear. But

---

4. *Parashat Ekev.*
5. Num. 10:9.

the Torah also commands that the same *hatzotzrot* produce the long, continuous sounds of *tekia* in joyful accompaniment to the bringing of our offerings in the Temple. Here it is used as an instrument of love. On Rosh HaShana, of course, we combine both *tekia* and *terua*, making fear and love equally important paths to the *devekut* we seek. The shofar itself is linked to both. It inspires awe: "Will a shofar be sounded in a city and the people not tremble?"[6] It also figures in the pomp and ceremony surrounding the coronation of a king. We signify with great love and joy our yearly coronation of the King through the *tekia*.

For all its seriousness, we do not treat Rosh HaShana with cold sobriety. Still listening to the ancient command of Nehemya, we treat Rosh HaShana like a holiday in regard to the clothes we wear and the festive meals we consume. *Devekut* cannot coexist with feelings of depression and futility. (The shedding of tears prescribed by the Ari must come from a sense of longing for God, not from depression and futility.) The holiday conduct is an adjunct to developing the sought-after *devekut*; it rides a crest of *bitahon* in God's mercifulness.

Devekut, though, is such a tall order! How do we get there, especially at a time when we are unusually aware of our misdeeds and shortcomings? A marvelous parable guides us. A lowly soldier stands in wait, part of the honor guard along the route that the king is expected to travel. The king's arrival is significantly delayed. Being a hot day, the soldier uses the extra time to freshen up. He sheds his clothes and takes a dip in the river. Unexpectedly, he hears the king's entourage approaching quite rapidly. This plunges him into a state of confusion and doubt. Hardly in a state to receive the king, he considers that he should perhaps hide himself. On the other hand, his job calls for him being on hand to honor the king.

He decides that he simply cannot lose the opportunity to receive the king, and he stands naked and exposed at his post. While others are horrified, the king discerns that his subject's behavior proves that he regards the honor of the king as more important than his own shame and embarrassment. Instead of punishing him as his advisors suggest, aghast at the bizarre sight, he bestows a medal upon the soldier for his

---

6. Ibid. 10:10.

devotion. This is our job exactly – to present ourselves before the King on Rosh HaShana. Despite seeing ourselves as naked and exposed, we must nonetheless appear at His coronation and appeal to His compassion, hoping that our service will be lovingly accepted.

Our approach helps show why an apparent inequity is not what it seems to be. "He perceives no sin in Yaakov and saw no perversity in Yisrael."[7] God, of course, sees everything. If He fails to notice the faults of Jews, it can only be that He decides that He will not see! This is hardly fair. Is it not inconsistent with His justice that He should play favorites?

The continuation of the verse is sometimes invoked to provide an explanation: "Hashem his God is with him." The sin of a Jew is never a full-blown act of rebellion and defiance. A proper Jew never manages to squeeze the full experience of sinning out of the act. He may capitulate to his evil inclination in a moment of weakness, but even as he sins, his pleasure is curtailed. He never quite maximizes on the experience. While in the very process of transgression, he already feels stung by the sense of betraying Hashem, of disobeying the God whom he loves. Thus he is robbed of the excitement of complete immersion in sin.

Our approach, however, offers an alternative explanation. The verse suggests a different truth about our behavior. Even after committing some sin, "Hashem... is with him." A Jew rebounds from his indiscretions and finds a way to renew his connection, to reestablish his *devekut* with God.

Devekut is the antidote to so much of what is wrong about us. *Devekut* to God purifies us, brings atonement to us. Sin simply cannot coexist with the presence of God. Its inherent deficiency is incompatible with His perfection. Those burdened by awareness of their considerable flaws will find solace in this. *Devekut* is indeed possible for us on Rosh HaShana, and in it we will find the way to surmount what we do not like or accept about ourselves.

---

7. Num. 23:21.

The Greatest Gift of All

I have forgiven, because of your words."[1] Three times in rapid succession we shout this line, precisely as we usher in the holiest day of the year. The phrase seems perfectly appropriate for our needs – just the message we want to hear. But is it not a bit presumptuous? Are we perhaps jumping the gun, projecting ahead of ourselves what we hope to secure in a period of intense service of God? Shouldn't these words come at the end of Yom Kippur, after a full day of fasting, repentance, confession, and prayer?)

Moreover, upon reflection, the message conveyed by the phrase is not as positive as we think. Consider the words that follow immediately: "But as I live... all the men who have seen My glory... and have tested Me these ten times and have not heeded My voice, they will see the land that I have sworn to give their forefathers – and all who anger Me shall not see it."[2] God's forgiveness was not a free pass. It came at a huge price. In essence, God told those who had accepted the report of

---

Based on *Netivot Shalom* 2:171–172.

1. Num. 14:20.
2. Ibid. 14:22–23.

the spies that they were indeed forgiven, but they were going to have to pay a stiff penalty, one that would last many years.

Is this the divine answer we wish to hear on Yom Kippur? Don't we really want to hear, "You are forgiven, the slate has been wiped clean, and the forecast for the coming year is sunny and bright"? We would like to hear an unequivocal "Surely!" in response to our appeal for all things good for ourselves and our families. It is curious that we lead off our Yom Kippur prayers with an apparent "You are forgiven – but with reservations."

Yet another familiar bit of phraseology seems to lose its luster when we ponder it. "Rabbi Akiva said, 'How fortunate are you, Israel. Before whom do you purify yourselves, and who purifies you? – your Father in heaven!'"[3] What exactly does it tell us? Who else would we think could purify us?

We will make headway with these problems only if we break out of our usual thought patterns. We might start by recognizing that the chief function of Yom Kippur is not forgiving sin, or granting atonement, or sundry other ways of describing a slate wiped clean.

Why should God announce a yearly amnesty, available to all who are fortunate enough to be Jewish? At all other points in the year, we deny that God simply excuses wrongdoing – "Whoever claims that God disregards wrongdoing, his own life shall be disregarded."[4] Does He break His rules on Yom Kippur?

Let's go back to the aftermath of the sending of the spies, and the people's rejection of the land. God's first reaction was, "I will smite them with a plague and annihilate them, and I will make you a greater and more powerful nation than they."[5] In other words, God was prepared to sever the special relationship with the Jewish people. He would abandon them, cast them off. His plans for history would continue through a new people, to be built from Moshe's progeny.

Moshe's prayers succeeded in aborting that plan; God relented and said, "I have forgiven, because of your words." God was ready to take

---

3. Yoma 85b.
4. Bava Kamma 50a.
5. Num. 14:12.

the Jewish people back in, so to speak. Their sin would not be overlooked. It would be dealt with – but they would not be left standing outside in the spiritual cold. They would not suffer the fate they feared the most – utter rejection by their Creator.

What a relief for them to hear that they were no longer locked out of His presence! Only one scenario is unbearable to a believing Jew: complete banishment from before God. We begin Yom Kippur by drawing on God's words from that episode over three thousand years ago, which represent His pledge never to fully abandon any Jew. We remind ourselves that each of us stands inside, in His presence, rather than outside. It is the perfect beginning – not end – of our Yom Kippur. With this reassurance, we can begin the service of the holiest day of the year. We can take advantage of its gift, and leave a day later on a more elevated plane.

In beginning that first service of God, the words of Rabbi Akiva become important. Through our soul-searching in Elul, and as the Days of Awe draw closer, our malaise increases. Discomfort morphs into real fear. The greatest fear for many is that we have botched things so badly that, consciously or subconsciously, we conclude that we cannot speak openly to God. From where will we find the *ḥutzpa* to stand before Him and plead for mercy once again? Sullied as we are by sin, caked in the mud of wrongdoing from head to toe, can we really walk into a Yom Kippur and function properly?

Rabbi Akiva provides the antidote to our paralysis. Before whom do we seek forgiveness on Yom Kippur? Before our Father! Our Father will let us in the front door, even caked in mud! He will accept us with our inadequacies, just as he did in the infancy of our peoplehood. This is what fathers do when their children stand at the doorstep, with only their eyes indicating that they seek reconciliation.

Reconciliation, then, is the magic word to describe the power of Yom Kippur. But this does not sound entirely accurate either. The Torah calls it a day of atonement, not a day of reconciliation. Aren't they very different? In truth, however, reconciliation and atonement are not distant relatives but close cousins.

Tanna DeVei Eliyahu[6] tells us that God's cleansing of Jewish sins gives Him great joy. Think of a king who becomes embroiled in a bitter

---

6. Ch. 1.

dispute with his son. There is pain on both sides, although that of the son does not compare to that of the father. If father and son make up, their former bitterness helps propel their love to something stronger than what it was before their pained separation.

It is good for both of them to be together again. It is even better for the father than for the son. That is just part of what it is to bear children, to be a parent. God reacts the same way, as it were. He savors the reconstituted bond between Himself and His people. He acts to bolster and support it. To make it work well, He throws in the ultimate deal sweetener. He generously grants amnesty to His beloved children, complete with atonement and purification. Atonement is not the essence of the day but its by-product. Reconciliation remains the central motif; atonement follows in its wake.

Only a parent acts with such unstinting generosity. This is precisely Rabbi Akiva's point. Before whom do we purify ourselves? Before our Father! A father who forgives is not the same as a friend or neighbor who forgives. In the case of our heavenly Father, the welcome-back of reconciliation brings with it the bonus of purification.

But how do we get ourselves to show up at the door? Is simply living through the day of Yom Kippur sufficient? To some degree, it is. If we understand what it should mean, though, we can take away from the day far more.

Here, too, the words of Rabbi Akiva allude to the fuller answer. Before whom do we purify ourselves? Before our heavenly Father. Let us recall who our Father is. Our diminutive minds are capable of grasping nothing of His essence. The smallness we feel can be painful. We might think of shrinking away, of drawing back from the power of His presence.

A better strategy would be to seek refuge, to find a place of safety. For believing Jews, not only is there such a place, but we are all familiar with its address. We escape not by running away but by rushing headlong directly into Him. We submerge our smallness into His greatness. We negate our own importance and reach out to cling to Him. By negating ourselves, by negating our sense of self, He moves within range. *Bittul* is the key to achieving *devekut*. (The Torah alludes to this in its description of the Yom Kippur service in the Holy of Holies: "No person shall be in the Tent of Meeting when he comes to provide atonement in the Sanctuary."[7] At this moment of encounter with the Divine, one ceases to be a person. He must translate his inadequacy and smallness into a self-negation that leads directly to *devekut* with God. He must leave the limitations of his humanity behind and become one with God.

The thought is not a new one. The Maharal[8] uses it to explain how Yom Kippur works. It is a day that the souls of Jews find their way back to their Source. Through self-negation, the soul merges back into God.[9] Within God, sin has no place. It is not that sin is left at the door. Rather, the soul is cleansed of the sin that adheres to it by now clinging to Something that simply does not allow sin to exist.

Interestingly, there is a parallel to this in an activity far more common than the once-yearly service of Yom Kippur. Rabbi Akiva introduces another image: "Just as a *mikve* purifies the impure, so does the Holy One, blessed be He, purify Yisrael." Think of what we are doing and saying when we immerse in a *mikve*. We submerge ourselves – completely and absolutely – in the water, becoming part of it. No small part of ourselves remains outside. Before we enter, we remove any substances that interpose between our bodies and the water. Through the Maharal, we understand this idea. A *mikve* purifies those submerged in it. On Yom Kippur, God helps us submerge ourselves, lose our egos, nullify our sense of self through complete union with Him.

Great rebbes used to speak on Erev Yom Kippur about *mesirut nefesh*, giving our lives for God. Why? What does dying for the sanctification of God's name have to do with Yom Kippur? They would plead with the congregation: "Why should we have to live though all sorts of consequences and punishment for our misdeeds? Visualize yourself in

---

7. Lev. 16:17.

8. *Derush LeShabbat Teshuva*, 83–85. In the Temple, this was demonstrated by taking the blood of the goat designated by lot "for God" and bringing it into the Holy of Holies. The blood represents the Jewish soul, or *neshama*; bringing it inside makes the statement that the immediate source from which that *neshama* is taken, and to which it now returns, is God Himself.

9. Curiously, the etymology of "atonement" supports this approach. The word comes to us through the Middle English term "atonen," which in turn comes from "at one."

your heart of hearts as if you were giving your life for God, and that will substitute for all sorts of unpleasantness."

Mesirut nefesh is nothing more than a demonstration of *bittul*. It is a statement that one's own needs, interests, goals, desires – none of them matter, relative to what God wants. It is the submerging of the most powerful instinct – survival – into the reality of God. When a sinner achieves such self-negation, there is no further purpose in punishing him for his sins. By becoming one with God, the sinner has disappeared completely and naturally – at that point, he ceases to be a man. His face shines with the radiance of the angels, but mortal man he is no longer.

What an outstanding opportunity Yom Kippur offers us – the ability to become nothing! Arriving there, we find not absence, but the ultimate Presence. We return to God in the mutual joy of reconciliation. Of the myriad divine gifts of which we are conscious, it may be the greatest gift of all.

Sukkot

Renewing God's Lease

Ono last chance.

No one likes to hear that ultimatum, but usually it is better than not having any last chance at all. In the messianic future, our Sages tell us,[1] as the rest of the world begins to figure out the new terms for a changed world, the nations ask the Holy One, blessed be He, to include them in the future delights. Informed that those are reserved for those who worked for them for the last millennia, they are sorely disappointed. God offers them one last chance: sukka.

Why sukka? We begin by examining one of the themes of the holiday.

Shabbat and Sukkot strike us as an unlikely partnership. To be sure, each Sukkot holiday contains its Shabbat. But it also contains a Sunday and Monday. And Passover does the same. If we pointed out that the first letters of the Torah's instruction to dwell in sukkot ("*basukkot teshvu shivat yamim*," "in sukkot you shall dwell seven days") are an anagram for "Shabbat," it would begin to shed light on the connection between the two.

Based on *Netivot Shalom* 2:200, 202–203.

1. Avoda Zara 2a.

We could build on this by observing that our Sages[2] teach that one who ushers in Shabbat with the recitation of the *vayekhulu* passage – the Torah's description of the first Shabbat after Creation – becomes a partner with God in the Creation enterprise. That is a fairly rare approbation.[3] It turns up in connection with Sukkot as well.[4] But we would still not be convinced that there was anything to the connection unless we demonstrate some logical link.

We might begin by examining the reason for Creation. One of the better-known approaches to the question posits that "God desired a dwelling place in the lower worlds."[5] We understand this to mean that man can make room for God, so to speak, in a world that is not only far removed from the essence of God but in some ways the opposite. Our world is entirely physical, which means that it is constrained, bounded, limited – and physicality is the opposite of God's limitlessness. Even the spiritual forces present in the world can be corrupt. God, on the other hand, is transcendent, holy, and pure.

Nonetheless, we do carve out a place for His presence in three different spheres: place, time, and soul. No one and no thing can accomplish this other than man. When we succeed, we become partners with Him in Creation, because we enable Him, in a manner of speaking, to achieve His objective.

As the new year begins, God wishes not only that we utilize our time more properly but that we assist in revisiting and renewing His purpose in Creation. Sukkot gives us the opportunity to create His dwelling place in each of the three possible areas.[6] The seven-day festival itself creates a "place" in time. Our taking of the four species attempts to sanctify every different part of ourselves and thus invites God into our core beings.

The most dramatic way in which we create space for Him is in the realm of space; we do so through the mitzva of sukka. In it we create

---

2. Shabbat 119b.
3. Our Sages do employ it in regard to judges who judge properly (Shabbat 10a) and those who safeguard the holiness of the holidays (*Pesikta Zutreta, Pinḥas*).
4. *Be'er Heitev, Oraḥ Ḥayim*, 639.
5. Numbers Rabba 13:6.
6. See the next chapter, "Outfitters for the Yearly Expedition."

an environment so welcoming to holiness that the *Ushpizin*, the Seven Shepherds of our people – Avraham, Yitzḥak, Yaakov, Moshe, Aharon, and David – feel comfortable joining us. Living our very human lives in its rarefied atmosphere, we elevate the ordinary events of eating, drinking, sleeping, and conversing and give them a role in hosting the Divine Presence.

The sukka recreates our early history, when we were surrounded by the Clouds of Glory – which also housed the Divine Presence. Indeed, when the Torah makes it imperative to join memory with mitzva performance on Sukkot ("So that your generations will know that I emplaced the Benei Yisrael in sukkot when I took them out of Egypt"), it means to underscore this common theme of the sukka and the Clouds of Glory – the presence of God in their midst. (The Zohar[7] is effusive in its praise of the generation of the Exodus – the *dor de'ah*, the generation of understanding. The depth of their comprehension was owed to their living within the Clouds of Glory. The proximity to God's presence matured their minds and gave clarity and insight.

We return to our original question. When the nations ask to join in receiving the perks of the messianic age, among them will be many of the righteous gentiles. They will not have rejected God, neither through disbelief nor sloth. They will understand that Torah and mitzvot – which they missed out on – are the best ways for a person to serve Him.

They will not understand, however, what sukka is all about. They will not relate to the idea that ordinary human activities can become so positive that they contribute to providing a place for the *Shekhina*. God gives them the mitzva of sukka and then causes the sun to shine so fiercely that they abandon the sukka and kick it in disgust on the way out.

The heat that they experience is the welling up of the evil inclination, which is almost unavoidable in the course of living through ordinary human activities. The non-Jews give up on the attempt. How can they possibly create a comfort zone for the *Shekhina* when they cannot leave their material selves behind? How can human activity possibly be elevated when it never relents on miring us in lesser thoughts and

---

7. Zohar 3:168b.

pursuits? They turn on this attempt to elevate everyday pursuits as an exercise in futility.

Indeed, our very humanity virtually guarantees that we cannot constantly direct our thoughts to higher purposes alone. Everyone's evil inclination gets in the way. When that happens, we cannot achieve the lofty purpose of the sukka. We Jews as well are compelled to leave it behind.

Conceded, says the Gemara. But when we leave, we don't kick it. When a Jew falls prey to his evil inclination he does not give up on the *avoda* of elevating the ordinary. He refuses to abandon the mission. He looks at his failure with shame and embarrassment – but not resignation.

Sometimes he succeeds in directly accomplishing the elevation of ordinary living. But even when his limitations prevent him – even when he leaves the sukka – his broken heart itself becomes an altar to God.

Outfitters for the Yearly Expedition

So much happens; so little is said.

The Torah tells us much about what we are supposed to do on Sukkot, with its full inventory of mitzvot. It is remarkably tight-lipped about explaining or characterizing the nature of the holiday. It instructs us how to mark the days but not what they are about. After introducing the festival of Sukkot[1] the Torah finds it sufficient to say, "You shall celebrate Hashem's festival for a seven-day period"[2] without letting us know what it is that we are celebrating! We are told as well that it involves seven days of simḥa,[3] of rejoicing, but we are left in the dark about what it is that should make us rejoice.

We can only conclude that the two special mitzvot of the season – sukka, the four species – plus the seven days of the holiday itself make up the very essence of the festival. Rather than dwell on how they differ

---

Based on *Netivot Shalom* 2:193–194.

1. Lev. 23:34.
2. Ibid. 23:39.
3. Ibid. 23:40.

from each other, we should look for the commonality that makes them perfect celebration-mates.

Our search begins with the *Torat Avot's* explication of the Torah's description of Sukkot elsewhere:[4] "the ingathering festival, *tekufat hashana*, at the year's circuit."[5] Now any occurrence that is regular and yearly marks a circuit. Only one season, however, strikes us as important for ushering in a new unit after concluding an old one. Sukkot seems to be part of the way in which we introduce a new unit of calendrical time. The *Torat Avot* explains that it provides us with *tekifut* – the resolve and strength we need for the service of God in the new year. We shop for the tools we need to do our jobs in the months ahead.

We equip ourselves with a heightened connection to holiness. The three parts of Sukkot – the sukka, the seven days of the holiday, and the four species – correspond to the three varieties of holiness that we encounter as Jews: place, time, and person. Sukkot arms us with greater ability to seed holiness in every place where it can take root.

With the sukka, we practice creating holy space. For a week, we spurn the accoutrements of a life of comfort and leave our homes. We take up residence in the simplicity of a sukka, which we build in order to spend quality time with God without the distractions of our usual material interests. This willingness allows us to create a holy space, separate from all others, one in which the *Ushpizin* are welcome. We understand why the Gemara[6] says that just as the name of heaven is associated with the days of Sukkot, so is it joined to the sukka itself – it becomes holy.

The weeklong holiday is an exercise in sanctifying time. We isolate the seven days and elevate them in holiness.

We are taught that the four species correspond to different parts of the body. The mind, heart – indeed, all our bodily components – join in the execution of the mitzva. They declare that all parts of ourselves – even our physical selves – give valuable assistance to our souls in the

---

4. Ex. 34:22.
5. Rashi sees *tekufa* as coming from cycle and circuit. The *Targum* sees it as the going out, or changing, of the year, meaning the old year changing to the new.
6. Sukka 9a.

execution of our personal missions. When all our abilities are coordinated in the service of God, they sing a beautiful harmony accompanying the melody of our souls. We find holiness in the focused purposefulness of ordinary living.

Having practiced the creation of holiness in all realms, we are prepared to keep at it the rest of the year. Now that we understand how the three parts of Sukkot converge to sharpen our skills in the service of God, we are no longer troubled by a strange phrase: "You shall celebrate it as a festival for Hashem, a seven-day period *in the year.*"[7] The Torah here gives voice to what we have said. The purpose of Sukkot is to equip us with the spiritual tools we need to make a difference in the new year. The threefold exercise in creating holiness does just that.

---

7. Lev. 23:41.

Taking the Lulav
on Shabbat

Unity themes abound regarding the four species. Different
midrashim emphasize different aspects, but the common denominator
is that they see unity growing out of plurality. The four may represent
different parts of the body, or different kinds of Jews, but the bottom
line is the same. The many are bidden to come together and form a uni-
fied collective.

This approach is a favorite source of discussion on Sukkot, but
its logic is not immediately compelling. What does it have to do with
Sukkot more than other times of the year? Additionally, the Torah
specifies what the four species are supposed to do for us. We are told
to rejoice with them when we take them. How does the unity theme
give rise to rejoicing?

If we understand Sukkot to be a complement to the Days of Awe,
the pieces fall into place. We have already established that the point of
Rosh HaShana is to coronate the King, to fully realize and accept the
authority of God in our lives. During the first part of the month of

Based on *Netivot Shalom* 2:203–206.

Tishrei we work on this through the modality of *yira*, or approaching God through a sense of reverence. On Sukkot, we do the same, this time using the tools of love of God.

More specifically, Sukkot is the time when we can turn the kingship of God from an abstraction to a reality vested in every part of our being. This is the significance of the four species as representations of the different parts of the body. Cleansed of our shortcomings on Yom Kippur, we can internalize His kingship in all parts of ourselves. On Sukkot, as at no other time of the year, we put our newly won purity to good use, applying it through love of God to accomplish what *yira* alone did not do. The first day of Sukkot is linked to Avraham, the first of the *Ushpizin*, whose *middot* are ḥesed and love. (The Torah alludes to the role of love in juxtaposing the mitzva of the four species with that of happiness: "And you shall take on the first day… and rejoice."[1] Proper love comes after and is built upon *yira*; through it, we can get to genuine joy.) While we may fail in attempts to achieve the clarity of purpose at other times of the year, Sukkot – with its gift of happiness and love – can get us there. We arrive at a place where we can genuinely feel, "All my limbs will say, 'Hashem, who is like You?'"[2]

A different midrash provides a variation on the unity theme. Each of the four species, it notes, comes with a different basket of assets and deficits. When taken together, one compensates for what the next lacks. We can view this as a guide to life's challenges. The Maharal teaches[3] that wholeness and perfection come in three varieties. True perfection comes only if we are perfect in our relationship to God, to others, and to ourselves. Like the four species, life provides situations that have *taam verei'aḥ*, taste and aroma, while others have one or the other. Some situations have neither.

This holds true for each of the areas of perfection. At times, God makes His presence and closeness felt, and we sense the richness in serving Him. At other times, He withholds part of the experience, as if we could detect the taste but not the aroma, or the opposite. There

---

1. Lev. 23:40.
2. Ps. 35:10.
3. *Ḥiddushei Aggados*, Bava Kamma 30a.

are also times when we feel nothing, making it much harder on us. Our job, however, is to serve Him as the absolute King, regardless of how He presents Himself to us. Like the *eved Ivri* – the indentured servant of Exodus 21 – we are to work day and night, whether He illuminates our lives or leaves us in the dark.

Our relationships with others are governed by the same lack of uniformity. Some people appeal to us in all aspects, while others offer at least some likable characteristics. Still others do not excite us in any way at all. Nonetheless, we are expected by the Torah to love all Jews, regardless of how much or how little they appeal to us.

Similarly, we face mood changes that threaten the way we relate to ourselves. At the extreme, some people are constantly in the thrall of the vicissitudes of life and their own mood changes. The amount of satisfaction they take out of life is constantly in flux, depending on their mood and how much enthusiasm they can muster for the moment. Peace and tranquility evade them. They can become fundamentally dissatisfied with themselves. Here too, accepting the kingship of God in its fullness demands that we not slip into moroseness and lethargy but rise above our natural feelings. We must remain satisfied with ourselves and the circumstances that God deals us, confident that everything God sends our way furthers His plan and purpose. This allows us to bear all burdens with joy and love.

The message of the four species – the lesson that this mitzva was designed to impart to our souls – is that all types and situations require the same response from us. Some may be more difficult or more attractive for us than others, but we are required nonetheless to remain steadfast and consistent in our pursuit of perfection in all our relationships, whether to God, to others, or to ourselves. From the diversity of qualities in the four species, we arrive at a point of uniformity.

Uniformity is desirable in other areas as well. We can experience firm belief and faith in God with different parts of ourselves. *Emuna*, belief, exhibits itself across a continuum, ranging from cerebral *emuna*, *emuna* of the heart, to *emuna* which takes hold of every fiber of a person's being. The same distinctions apply to *devekut*. We can cling to God with our minds alone, or with our feelings and heart, or with everything that is in us. The four species beckon us – and help us along the way – to attach ourselves to Him with all that we have, not just with one faculty or aspect of ourselves. On Sukkot we find that we have become a choir of different instruments, all ready to sing His praises.

This internal uniformity in our *devekut* leads us directly to joy and exultation. While happiness is part of the celebration of every holiday, on Sukkot it is the overarching quality of the entire week. We call it *zeman simḥatenu*, the season of our joy. The joy of uniform *devekut* to God, *devekut* with all parts of ourselves, is not another element of the holiday but its very essence.

If our approach has merit, we can understand why our Sages were prepared to sacrifice a mitzva that occurs but once a year because of what seems like a remote possibility of Shabbat violation. They may not have sacrificed anything at all when they suspended the mitzva of taking the four species on Shabbat, for fear that people would carry them in the public domain.

Shabbat is called *yoma denishmata* – the day of the soul. Shabbat is characterized by the twin mitzvot of *zakhor* and *shamor*, or remembering and guarding. The latter is observed passively, while the former is an affirmative obligation, like so many more in the Torah. Yet the vast majority of *mitzvot aseh*, affirmative obligations, call for some sort of activity. *Zakhor*, however, requires only speech. Another way of looking at this is that on Shabbat – the day of the soul – speech alone can accomplish what requires concrete action the rest of the week. Shabbat actualizes what is otherwise only potential.

The mitzva of the four species ordinarily requires a physical activity to help us assimilate God's kingship in every part of our being, or attach ourselves to Him with every dimension of ourselves, or learn to blink at all the curveballs thrown at us. On Shabbat, we do the same without the physical lulav and etrog. The lesson becomes part of us even without grasping the species in our hands. We do not sacrifice the mitzva so much as engage it more internally.

Whether with the real lulav and etrog or Shabbat's virtual kind, the holiday of Sukkot helps us bring together different strands and turn them into a single, strong cord.

The Greatness of the Last *Hoshana*

"**P**lace me like a seal on Your heart, like a seal on Your arm. For strong till the death is my love."[1]

These words, says the *Beit Avraham*, bring Yom Kippur and Hoshana Rabba together. Both of these days are end points and conclusions. With Yom Kippur we end the Days of Awe, in which we pour out our hearts – our internal selves – to God in prayer. Hoshana Rabba brings to a close the season richest in practical mitzvot like sukka and the four species. The arm, through which we reach out and manipulate our surroundings, serves as a symbol of external activity; in this case, it symbolizes the performance of mitzvot.

Why do we invoke the image of seals? Because a seal connotes binding finality. It is not unusual for us to speak and write about intentions and plans. We obligate ourselves, however, only when the ink dries on a formal agreement, sealed by our signature. We find ourselves in an analogous position in our service of God. We wish and yearn for many

---

Based on *Netivot Shalom* 2:210–213.

1. Song. 8:6.

spiritual things. Who among us does not wish to grow in his *yira*, his fear of God? When the Days of Awe are upon us, every committed Jew wishes to change and pledges to conduct himself differently.

Our earnest intentions do not always produce a signed agreement. With time, too many of our resolutions and pledges weaken. So do the contrition of repentance and the zeal of a new beginning. As a Jew prepares to take leave of the Days of Awe and Sukkot, he must think in terms that are concrete and resolute. He must be ready to make absolute and unyielding commitments.

"God has made the one as well as the other."[2] God acts toward us exactly as we conduct ourselves toward Him. The quality of the seal with which we conclude our intense weeks of introspection and repentance determines how our fate is sealed above. Is our resolve tentative, or are we determined to keep our end of the bargain, regardless of what time will bring?

Hoshana Rabba – as the seal of the active, performance-oriented part of the season – prefigures the way we will be treated in the year to come. Are we prepared to alter our actions so that all parts of ourselves are pressed into His service? Our individual seals are significant only if they encompass both active and inner components – both the "arm" and the "heart."

The way we are judged is completely dependent upon us. The *Toldot Yaakov Yosef* explains that the famous three books described in the Gemara[3] are not records of our past behavior. Rather, they are projections for the future. What kind of person has he resolved to be in the next year? A righteous person – or otherwise? Each person is placed before these books, pen in hand, and asked to sign where he wishes. If he commits himself to act in the future as an absolutely righteous person, he is immediately written and sealed for a year of good life. If he finds it completely impossible to make any change at all, then the very opposite occurs.

Matters of the heart are sometimes hidden even from ourselves. Some inner matters remain entirely closed off to us, giving us very little

---

2. Eccl. 7:14.
3. Rosh HaShana 16b.

ability to master them. For this reason, the seal of action is so crucial, and the seal of the heart on Yom Kippur is insufficient. After a week of performing the mitzva of the four species (symbolizing, as they do, all the different parts of the human body), we stand on Hoshana Rabba with our actions purified, ready to be different people in the coming year. Through this, we merit being sealed for a year of good.

The Zohar[4] describes the transition between Hoshana Rabba and Shemini Atzeret as moving from judgment to blessing, from days of judgment to a festive and joyful celebration to which the King invites none other than His special people, and at which no requests to Him are denied.

This scenario suggests a different reading of the verse from the Song of Songs with which we opened. The two seals might be Hoshana Rabba and Shemini Atzeret. Each is a kind of *Ne'ila*. Hoshana Rabba concludes the season of divine judgment and our service of God through fear. Shemini Atzeret brings our time of rejoicing, and its attention to divine love, to its close.

Close friends who must part often ply each other with reminders of their friendship to keep their bond fresh and vital in times of separation. God, too, gives us different protocols to remind us of our closeness. Hoshana Rabba encapsulates the concrete, practical activities of the days that preceded it – the special mitzvot of Sukkot, or the "arm" once again. Shemini Atzeret serves as a reminder of the love, the "heart," generated by all the days of joy and rejoicing during the week of Sukkot.

Both forms are necessary, since each alone is incomplete. The stirrings of our heart are often changeable and sometimes distant from our own consciousness. We do not always serve God with feeling, enthusiasm, and unbridled love. At times, our hearts feel choked off.

Actions, too, have their shortcomings. On the one hand, they can be called upon whenever appropriate and are thus more dependable than feelings. On the other hand, however, actions without attendant feelings are incomplete and hollow. Only the two acting together – hearts and arms – properly bind a person to God and insure that we serve Him as we should.

---

4. Zohar 3:32a.

The *Mateh Moshe* observes that Hoshana Rabba's calendar date is always 21 Tishrei. Twenty-one is the *gematria* of one of God's names: "I Will Be."[5] This name speaks of the future. As such, it is the characteristic of God which allows repentance, or the ability of a person to make a new beginning, to become something new, to look only to the future and discard the past.

While regretting the past is also part of the repentance process, it is clearly the determination of the future which spells the difference between successful and unsuccessful repentance. Rabbi Aharon Karliner reported an interaction with a repentant individual. "I simply could not speak with him on a common wavelength. He spoke only of rectifying the past. I wanted only that he should accept upon himself the future."

The person who remains essentially the old sinner that he was is incapable of making any real commitment to the future. How could he? Of what value is a declaration about the future when all the old causes for failure are still in place? For this reason, we have a month of Elul. After weeks of introspection and soul-searching, we can put aside some of our past on Rosh HaShana.

Some need to travel a greater distance. Such a person may not find himself sufficiently changed on Rosh HaShana. He is not yet ready to become a different person. For him, the Ten Days of Repentance offer another opportunity for self-transformation. Still others have a longer way to go. For them, Hoshana Rabba affords yet another chance. After a period of intense mitzva activity, of a week of serving God with extreme joy, it is a day ripe with opportunity to change through a repentance of love.

The greatness of Hoshana Rabba can be appreciated through a parable of the Rebbe of Ruzhin. A king exiled his one son from the palace. The prince took up with common folk, coarse and uncouth tillers of the soil. Gradually, he lost his princely polish and demeanor and became one of them. With the passage of time, the king became concerned for his son and sent a trusted advisor to find the prince and determine if he was in need of anything. The advisor was appalled to see the state into

---

5. Ex. 3:14.

which the prince had fallen but bit his lip and simply asked him whether he lacked anything that the king might send. The prince pondered for a moment and then replied that his boots had torn. Could the king perhaps send him a new pair of boots?

The advisor could no longer contain himself. He wept with compassion for the fallen state of the prince. "Your father is the king! He would give you anything. Can you think of nothing more than a pair of boots?"

Throughout the prayers of the Days of Awe, there is almost no mention of our earthly needs. The refrain we repeat calls instead for the magnification of God's honor and extension of His kingship. Yet, we are realistic. We realize that our vision is limited. We are all really far more interested in the smaller details of our mundane lives. The *Tikkunei Zohar*[6] holds nothing back: "They cry out like dogs! 'Give! Give! Give children; give life; give sustenance!'"

The Rebbe of Kobrin explains that it goes without saying that we should be crying out to God for our children, our lives, our sustenance. This is, after all, what praying is all about: throwing all our needs upon the Holy One, blessed by He. The requests are entirely appropriate. The passage criticizes us not for those requests but for our small-mindedness. We should not cry out like dogs who see nothing beyond their lowly existence. We should cry out because our needs are important to us in serving God.

But are we really there? Can we tell ourselves that we pray for lofty things, for God's name and honor, for His program in history? Don't we know what our innermost thoughts are and what we really seek from Him? If so, do we have the temerity to pray with one set of words when our intentions are quite different?

The prayers that accompany the *Hoshanot*, the special prayers of supplication, on Hoshana Rabba provide the answer. Notice how they are sequenced. We first cry out, "Save us, please!" Then we cry, "Save us, please; God, please save us." Finally, we elaborate: "Save us, God, indeed. You are our Father!" This reminds us of our prince, in a different frame of mind, determined to get back to the palace. He stands in

---

6. Zohar, *Tikkun* 6.

line, waiting to ask the beneficent monarch for help like all the others waiting to be heard. At first the king does not recognize him, and he asks and receives what all the other petitioners ask. While the others are satisfied, he keeps coming back for more, arguing that he is entitled to more. The king, exceedingly generous and compassionate, realizes that there is something unusual in the persistence of the requests. He approves them but asks for an explanation. At first the prince merely says that he is a member of the king's family and therefore privileged to ask for special treatment. After a while, the prince no longer contains himself. "It is I, your son! Don't you recognize me?"

When a Jew truly feels in his heart that God is his Father, when he no longer simply mouths the words, but their truth resonates deeply within, there is nothing that he cannot ask.

This is Hoshana Rabba, and this is its greatness. It is the day of the seal, the terminus of weeks of preparation, of repentance, of special mitzvot. It is the day that we can be inspired to our own greatness, to avert our gaze from the smaller agendas that usually preoccupy us. It is the time that we will not be satisfied with a new pair of boots, with the small things in life. It is the time that we can feel the closeness to Him and therefore in good conscience ask for the great salvation, for the solution to all problems of the individual and of the many.

Shemini Atzeret:
Wrapping It All Up

Y ou can't have it both ways. Unless you are Shemini Atzeret. Shemini Atzeret refuses to cooperate. It defies the accepted classification of *regalim*, the three holidays that required our presence in Jerusalem when we had a *Beit HaMikdash*. Shemini Atzeret, we are told,[1] is its own *regel*, a holiday unto itself. If so, however, there ought to be four *regalim*, not three. And it ought to be day one of that holiday, not day eight (which is of course the source of its name) of a different one. It also evades the pattern of other holidays which offer reasons for their celebration.

Except where they do not. Shemini Atzeret is definitely not alone in that regard. In fact, when we note which holidays are explained in the Torah and which are not, we detect a different pattern – which eventually leads us to a solution of our conundrum.

"Place me like a seal on Your heart, like a seal on Your arm... for strong till the death is my love."[2] The *Beit Avraham* notes that three

---

Based on *Netivot Shalom* 2:215–218.
1. Rosh HaShana 4b.
2. Song. 8:6.

regalim come with active elements. We eat matza on Passover, sound the shofar on Rosh HaShana, and dwell in the sukka on Sukkot. We celebrate their meaning by doing, symbolized by the arm, with which we actively manipulate objects in the world around us. Those holidays are the seal on the arm.

There are also three holidays in which we don't do anything at all. They are honored and appreciated internally. They are the seal on the heart, the locus of the love that is "strong till the death." They are more internal, more mysterious. (Two of them, Shavuot and Shemini Atzeret, offer no reason for their celebration. The third declares itself a day of atonement – but doesn't explain how or why.)

All three of this latter set prominently make use of the number eight. In the case of Shemini Atzeret, it is built in. Shavuot is also an eighth. It is the day not after seven but after seven times seven days following the beginning of Passover. At the climax of the service of Yom Kippur, the High Priest sprinkles blood in the Holy of Holies eight times – once directed above and seven below.

Eight is the number that evokes transcendence – one beyond seven, which represents all things in the physical world: the six days of Creation and the holiness of Shabbat that is fixed into the fabric of this existence. Eight speaks of a place that is beyond the limitations of this world – the Holy of Holies, in which our concept of space did not apply, and Torah itself, which comes from a place far loftier than our world.

And then there is Shemini Atzeret, which, explains the Ari, belongs more to the world after the final *tikkun*, the world of the final redemption, categorically different and removed from the one we now occupy.

To begin with, it comes after an entire season of intense activity but lacks an active element. It is part of the "heart" group rather than the "arm" group. We have built upon it the celebration of completing our yearly cycle of Torah reading. We read the final letter in the Torah, *lamed*, and then immediately we read the first letter of the Torah, *bet*; together these letters form the word *lev*, or heart.

Not only is Shemini Atzeret a member of that group, but one of its qualities makes it categorically different from the others and places it in a unique position. The key is the word *atzeret*, which means gathering or holding back. Shemini Atzeret gathers together and retains aspects of all that the other holidays of the year contributed.

Passover in no small part reflects God's boundless love for the Jewish people, without which He would not have reached out to an undeserving people and turned them into a Torah nation by way of a breathtaking succession of miracles. That love manifests itself in the dimension of Shemini Atzeret as a day of intimate connection between God and His people.[3] The seven days of Sukkot made room for the nations of the world, represented each day in the special *musaf* offerings. On Shemini Atzeret, the pattern of offerings shifts dramatically; only the Jewish people take part. After the big global event, God arranges a quieter, smaller affair for those with whom He is closest. The divine love of Passover shows itself in this final farewell get-together on Shemini Atzeret.

Rosh HaShana and Yom Kippur emphasize a different set of divine responses: those of judgment. These days of judgment remind us of His power and His justice, and strengthen our sense of fear rather than love. Those lessons are further distilled and brought to a final form on Shemini Atzeret, at the time of the "sealing" of the verdicts of the season of judgment. We come to understand the interrelationship between the divine characteristics of judgment and compassion, as Shemini Atzeret emphasizes the impact that the love of Sukkot has on raw judgment. By Shemini Atzeret, pure judgment has been tamed, "sweetened" by an admixture of *ḥesed*. So the Days of Awe find a home in Shemini Atzeret as well.

Finally, Shavuot – the time of the giving of the Torah – is also incorporated within Shemini Atzeret. We've turned the holiday into an annual celebration of finishing the yearly cycle of the public Torah reading. We react to it with an explosion of enthusiasm and love for the Torah we received at Sinai. We recognize that the way to take the lesson of Shavuot forward into the rest of the year is by lavishing on it love and joy.

Having come this far, we could suggest another reason for the Torah's silence about the purpose of Shemini Atzeret. The *Noam Elimelekh* suggests that the holiness of the white space of the Torah scroll

---

3. Sukka 55b.

is greater than what is formed by the ink that flows from the quill. The holiness of each character is linked to the inherent holiness of that letter; the holiness of the space in between knows the holiness of all letters.

Perhaps this is the way we should look at the calendar, at the holidays, at the three *regalim* and the fourth that is and is not joined to the others. All the special days of the year are like the letters of the Torah, each contributing its own meaning and holiness. Shemini Atzeret is the blank space that surrounds them – amorphous, mysterious, but bearing the imprint and holiness of all of them and more.

Shemini Atzeret: Taking *Daat* to the Limit

Y ou have to be pretty sure of yourself before reducing the description of a complex event to a single slogan. It gets even more complicated when that event itself is supposed to be a distillation of an entire system of events that precede it. The Rebbe of Kobrin, cited in *Torat Avot*, does just that in regard to Shemini Atzeret. In doing so, he allows us new insights into the nature of the day.

Passover is the first holiday of the year. That means that Sukkot is the last, and Shemini Atzeret is the last part of Sukkot. It also marks the conclusion of the Tishrei holidays, which have their own thematic platform. Somehow, Shemini Atzeret ties all these elements together. It revisits, condenses, summarizes, and provides a spiritual wallop with which to survive the next months.

The *Torat Avot* then distills this experience into a single lesson and finds the pithy language with which to express it. He locates it in a verse[1] with which we introduce the *hakafot* on Simḥat Torah: "You

---

Based on *Netivot Shalom* 2:218–219.
1. Deut. 4:35.

have been shown so that you will know that Hashem, He is God! There is nothing beside Him." All the lessons and experiences of the calendar year lead up to this realization on Shemini Atzeret. We will try to understand why this is so important, and how this understanding, cultivated over many months, comes to full bloom on this day.

The Ḥesed LeAvraham explains why Benei Yisrael succeeded in conquering lands of the seven nations that resided in ancient Israel but did not take actual possession of the land belonging to the full set of ten nations that had been promised to Avraham. The Keni, Kenizi, and Kadmoni did not fall to the advancing Jewish conquest. He explains that the ten nations represent the ten *sefirot*. Of those ten, seven are the more familiar active *sefirot*; the remaining three are the "intellects." They are not accessed through performance of mitzvot but through profound intellectual awakening.

Each of the *Ushpizin*, the Seven Shepherds, relates to one of the seven active *sefirot*. Each one of those guests in the sukka perfected one of the *sefirot*, making its content available to us. They did not do the same for the three *sefirot* mentioned above. It will take nothing less than the instruction of the Messiah to address the remaining *sefirot* and provide their *tikkun*. When that happens, title to the remaining three parcels of territory will fall to our hands.

This historical trajectory plays out on a smaller scale over the course of Sukkot. We invite the seven guests; each leaves us with his particular accomplishment. On Shemini Atzeret, we address the three remaining *sefirot*. In the words of the verse in Deuteronomy above, we are "shown" so that we will have *daat*. This *daat* is not a superficial knowledge about God's existence and His oneness. It is mastery, in part, of the knowledge that comes through a connection with God through the medium of the three loftiest *sefirot*: *ḥokhma*, *bina*, and *daat*.

While authorities dispute whether or not in our prayers we should attach the word *ḥag* to Shemini Atzeret as we do to the other holidays, the fact remains that the Torah's treatment of Shemini Atzeret is an anomaly. Nowhere does the Torah call Shemini Atzeret a *ḥag*. The word *ḥag* can be seen as an acronym for *ḥesed* and *gevurot*. All the other holidays are related to the lower seven *sefirot* that shuttle between (and contain elements of) the *middot* that fall under the rubrics of *ḥesed* and *gevura*. They all relate to the subtle interaction between spiritual characteristics that are expansive and outward directed (like *ḥesed* to its recipients) and those that restrain and impose limits (like *gevura*, also known as *din*) and are inward-focused. All of these, however, are sourced in the more ethereal upper *sefirot*, where there is only *ḥesed* and no *din* at all.

There always is a way to take away some lessons of immediate, practical value even when considering profound kabbalistic ideas. For a simple way to understand how Shemini Atzeret should impact our service of God, we return to the same verse in Deuteronomy. *"Ein od milvado,"* "There is nothing beside Him," is an expression of self-negation. We negate ourselves relative to the existence of God. While we try this at other times of the year utilizing different themes, on Shemini Atzeret we negate ourselves from a position of intense love of God, a product of the joy of the holiday of Sukkot. The verse speaks of being shown the exclusiveness of God through knowledge. *Daat* refers to an intense understanding that comes from complete merging and attachment, as in "Adam knew Ḥava his wife."[2]

True negation of self comes only with the keen knowledge that *ein od milvado*, that nothing can conceivably exist outside the existence of God. On Shemini Atzeret we strive to come to that realization.

---

2. Gen. 4:1.

Ḥanukka

The Holiday of *Emuna* and *Bitaḥon*

Each special day on the calendar contains a hidden dimension and therefore offers us its own gift. Our Sages[1] instruct us to "ask and inquire" about, or understand, the laws of those special days prior to their arrival. It also can be taken to mean that we are to turn to God and ask and inquire of Him to help comprehend the unique gift that each holiday brings to us. Where are they designed to take us? How do we ready ourselves for the journey? We must ask God for guidance as to how we should enter the holiday and what changes within us we can expect by living it fully.

Ḥanukka and Purim are the completion of the set of seven rabbinic mitzvot.[2] Added to the 613 mitzvot of the Torah, they form *keter* (whose *gematria* is 620), or "crown." *Keter* is the uppermost element of

---

Based on *Netivot Shalom*, Ḥanukka, 16–21.

1. See Megilla 4a.
2. There are of course hundreds of rabbinic fences and proscriptions. There are only seven affirmative rabbinic obligations. They include mitzvot such as most blessings, *eiruvin, netilat yadayim*, lighting candles for Shabbat and holidays, Hallel, Ḥanukka, and Megilla.

the ten *sefirot*. The system through which God's will is translated into concrete phenomena is completed only through the seven mitzvot that our Sages added to those of the Torah. Sensing the bitter and lengthy exile that Benei Yisrael would face after the Temple's destruction, our Sages provided these two holidays to accompany them on this terrible journey. Each year, these days would sustain us through our difficulties by shining upon us a light of *emuna* and *bitaḥon*.

Emuna, belief, and *bitaḥon*, trust, brought about our salvation at the founding events of each of these holidays. We awaited the implementation of a decree to physically destroy us at the time of the first Purim. The decree had been written and sealed with the seal of the King of kings. Any hope of survival at the time exceeded the ordinary and natural. We found *emuna* and *bitaḥon* that were beyond the ordinary. From it we drew our salvation. The same was true of Ḥanukka, where our spiritual existence was threatened and where once again we found *emuna* and *bitaḥon* where they could not have been expected to survive. From that *emuna* and *bitaḥon* we drew down the miracle from its heavenly source.

Our custom, says the *Magen Avraham*[3] is to repeat the last verse (*orekh yamim asbi'ehu*) when we recite *Yoshev BeSeter*[4] at the conclusion of Shabbat. As the *Tashbetz* points out, the repetition brings the word total to 130, which equals the numerical value of the term *hakohanim*, the priests. This chapter of Psalms was part of the arsenal of the Hasmonean priests. They went out to battle with it. It speaks of great trust in God without mentioning any merit on our part. It offers no bargaining chip to God and yet exudes confidence in Him. "My God – I will trust in Him!" The power of *bitaḥon* knows no limits.

Ironically, in one regard, Ḥanukka and Purim surpass the accomplishment of the Exodus from Egypt. There, drawing upon *emuna* alone, we were freed from the hand of our oppressor. At the time of Purim, however, we turned the tables on our enemies. Not only did we escape the designs of our oppressors, but we achieved dominion over them.[5] On Ḥanukka as well, we reestablished political independence for the

---

3. *Oraḥ Ḥayim* 295.
4. Ps. 91.
5. Est. 9:1.

next almost two hundred years.[6] In both of these cases, adding *bitaḥon* onto *emuna* made the difference.

In the final analysis, Torah and good deeds bring certain powers into play. Prayer adds other powers. Perched on top of both of them are *emuna* and *bitaḥon*, which provide access to the most potent of powers God sends our way. At times, we can feel that the power of our prayer is blunted, that various adversarial forces block the effectiveness of our prayers. These forces have no power, however, against *bitaḥon*. At such times, *emuna* and *bitaḥon* accomplish what prayer cannot.

Esther, entering the room that housed the royal collection of idols, felt the Divine Presence leave her.[7] Her reaction was to cry out to God. "My God, my God! Why have You deserted me?"[8] The next few verses[9] speak of her frustration as her prayers of both day and night prove ineffective. She then shifts to a stance of *bitaḥon* and finds renewed confidence. Where prayer does not work, *bitaḥon* still produces results.

The Gemara emphasizes that it was not until the one-year anniversary of the event that Ḥanukka was designated as a permanent observance. Why did our Sages wait a full year rather than act at the time the miracle occurred? Kabbalistic literatureexplains that our Sages had to determine whether the *or*, the special divine light that accompanied the miracle, would be a recurring one, or whether it was limited to its original occurrence. When they felt the light the following year, they knew that it would be a yearly event and the holiday became a permanent feature.

The original light did not shine down on us spontaneously. It was drawn down from its source through the trust of the priests who waged the battle against the Syrian-Greeks. It follows that the light that revisits us each year must be drawn to us through our *bitaḥon*.

This explains why the Gemara left us with three different levels of observing Ḥanukka: a basic level; *mehadrin*, that is, a more beautiful manner; and *mehadrin min hamehadrin*, the most beautiful manner. Our Sages offer us no parallel in any other mitzva. All of us perform every

---

6. *Mishneh Torah, Hilkhot Ḥanukka* 3:1.
7. Megilla 15b.
8. Ps. 22:2.
9. Ibid. 22:3, 5.

other mitzva according to a single set of expectations and demands. We can understand, though, that Ḥanukka must be exceptional. Since its all-important light becomes available to us only through our *emuna* and *bitaḥon*, there cannot be a single level of observance. *Emuna* and *bitaḥon* are infinitely nuanced. They are found in us on so many different levels; those differences are marked by different ways of fulfilling the mitzva of lighting.

Many are accustomed to reciting *Yoshev BeSeter* after lighting the Ḥanukka lights. The kabbalistic works see this as a function of the halakhic requirement of placing the menora within ten handbreadths of the ground. This lowest stratum of activity is seen in Kabbala as the province of the *ḥitzonim*, some of the dark spiritual forces. In other words, the darker spiritual forces are banished to the least elevated provinces of life. We place the Ḥanukka lights specifically there, to indicate that its light can penetrate the areas furthest removed from holiness. The attendant danger is that these forces that work against holiness can do much damage on their home turf. We therefore recite *Yoshev BeSeter*, one of whose themes is surviving the encounter with unforeseen dangers, both physical and spiritual. Its other theme is equally appropriate: we are saved from these hazards only through *bitaḥon* in God's intervention.

From where did the *bitaḥon* of the Hasmoneans come? The Torah says:[10] "You are children to Hashem." Just as the Torah is eternal and immutable, so is this statement. We never cease to be God's precious children. As the *Beit Avraham* points out, a king can show favor to a son for different reasons. If the son is particularly capable and accomplished, his father the king will take pleasure in his conduct and show favor to him. But it is likely that the king will show the most favor to a seriously disabled child, whose desperate straits awaken the compassion of his father, who realizes that the child depends on him entirely and exclusively. This child has no accomplishment or trait that would endear him to an unrelated, objective party. Parents, however, do not give up on their children and are moved by their helplessness.

Our redemption from Egypt is attributed to *emuna*. Benei Yisrael found themselves without merit, but they maintained their *emuna*

10. Deut. 14:1.

in their position as God's children. Thus, they knew they could rely on His mercy even when they found themselves with no special merit. The very same reaction supported our salvation in the victory of the Hasmoneans. As we say in the *Al HaNissm* prayer, "afterward, Your children came to the Holy of Holies of Your holy House." Recognizing themselves as God's children provided them with the *bitaḥon* that was answered by God granting them victory.

The Zohar invokes the verse "He relates the end from the beginning"[11] in commenting about *keter malkhut*, the organic connection between the first of the *sefirot, keter,* and the last, *malkhut. Keter,* in the final analysis, depends on *emuna,* the summation of all Torah and mitzvot. The "beginning" is the first of the Ten Commandments, which is *emuna.* Ironically, so is the "end," which is Ḥanukka, the last of the seven rabbinic mitzvot. Ḥanukka completes the crown. The journey that begins with the realization that "I am Hashem your God" ends in the display of the consequences of that relationship at Ḥanukka – showcasing the love He has for His children. Passover may be the Rosh HaShana, i.e., the most important day on the calendar for evidencing *emuna.* Similarly, Ḥanukka and Purim are the Rosh HaShana for displaying *bitaḥon.*

Our Sages fixed Ḥanukka for us to draw renewed *bitaḥon* in God each year from the light that lit our lives both in days of old and in our time.

---

11. Is. 46:10.

Song of Dedication

Forced to choose a single event that provided the impetus for declaring the holiday of Ḥanukka, most of us would point to the miracle of the lights. The oil that would not quit is an inescapable image of Ḥanukka and a dominant theme.

A different event, however, emerges in our literature as close competition. Surprisingly, it is this runner-up in the contest for significance that pulls ahead in the race and provides the name of the holiday. The miracle of the oil did not give Ḥanukka its name. The word "Ḥanukka" puts the other theme, that of dedication – or more accurately rededication – front and center. Why should this be?

Following the advice of Tractate Soferim,[1] we are accustomed to adding *Mizmor Shir Ḥanukkat HaBayit LeDavid*[2] to the prayers on Ḥanukka. This chapter of Psalms speaks of the dedication of some "house," but we don't readily understand to which "house" David refers. Some see it as the first *Beit HaMikdash*. The sundry ailments and near-fatal incidents to which David refers would then mean the exile and

---

Based on *Netivot Shalom*, Ḥanukka, 32–37.

1. Soferim 18:2.
2. Ps. 30.

travail that preceded its construction. But this is problematic, because the first *Beit HaMikdash* was not built after a period of exile and travail.

Others see David himself as the house; he speaks in appreciation of the restoration of his health and physical integrity. This is also difficult. *Tanakh* does not mention David struggling with a period of ill-health from which he recovered.

More likely is that David composed this prayer for every Jew who emerges from a period of pain and affliction, ready to rebuild the edifice of his spiritual core on the ruins of his former existence. The spiritual uncertainty of his old self is met with a psalm of rededication.

Our Sages did not immediately establish Ḥanukka as a permanent holiday. They waited a year to see if the light that graced the original event would return. When it did, they realized that the event had lasting significance. But they named the holiday after the rededication, not after the light. They understood that the function of the light was to provide light after an episode of complete despair. God had shown them that even in such bleak times, a small flask of purity remains with which to light the future. Ḥanukka became the time in which a Jew could confidently expect to rebuild his shattered inner house of spirituality. *Mizmor Shir* expresses the certainty that there are no grounds for absolute despair; at every moment of apparent abandonment by God, one should not hesitate to call upon Him for help.

If we still wish to anchor this psalm to the life of David, we should look to a period of spiritual, rather than physical, affliction. He wrote it, perhaps, in reaction to the episode with Batsheva, which itself is shrouded in difficulty. On the one hand, our Sages affirm that one who says that David sinned is mistaken;[3] on the other, they see David as having become leprous as a result of his crime and members of the Sanhedrin shunning him.[4]

There is no contradiction. David committed no vile wrong in an absolute sense. Relative to who he was and what spiritual level he

---

3. Shabbat 56a. According to this opinion, Batsheva was not a married woman, and Uriya was deserving of death as part of a defiant cabal that did not accept the authority of the king.

4. Yoma 22b.

occupied, however, his actions reflected a failing. He gives clear expression to this in the next psalm after *Mizmor Shir:* "I have sinned to You alone."[5] In other words, David's actions were not sinful in an absolute sense; they should not be perceived as sinful to others. But they were not perfectly congruent with what he knew to be God's will, and in that sense, they were an affront to Him alone.

There is a parallel in a story about the *Kadosh MeLublin,* who once faced a difficult challenge. In fighting his inner battle, he overlooked an actual halakhic objection. Not having that available, only one argument saved him from making the wrong choice. He resolved not to act without first determining that his conduct would bring pleasure, so to speak, to God. David meant the same. His sin was only to God in the sense that his actions did not bring pleasure to Him.

Our Sages[6] question the entire premise of *Mizmor Shir* that in its simple meaning speaks of the dedication of a house, which they take to mean the *Beit HaMikdash.* How could David speak of its dedication when it was not built in his lifetime? While David conceived of the project, it fell to his son to bring the plan to fruition. This, the Sages say, is largely irrelevant. David planned the construction of the Temple and would have seen it through to completion were it not for circumstances beyond his control. He is credited with its construction for the intent alone.

We can find an allusion in this to our primary theme. *Mizmor Shir* has universal application beyond the life of David, and its message is aimed at every Jew whose inner spiritual house totters on the brink of oblivion. It is a song of triumph for the Jew who has done the necessary repairs and improvements. It can be sung even by one who has longed for the changes, planned and designed them, even if he has not yet been successful in translating them into reality.

David is the symbol of messianic redemption. It is specifically he among the *Ushpizin*[7] whose line was chosen to produce the Messiah.

---

5. Ps. 51:6
6. *Shoḥer Tov* 30.
7. The three patriarchs, plus Yosef, Moshe, Aharon, and David, corresponding to the seven lower *sefirot.*

We give voice to this each month at *kiddush levana,* the monthly bless-ing of the New Moon, when we proclaim that David, king of Israel, is alive and enduring. From his earliest days, he experienced serial trag-edies and challenges. In his childhood he was derided and rejected by his brothers. Shaul believed that he was plotting against his life and pursued him with his forces. Becoming king after slowly and pain-fully consolidating his hold on the throne did not end his hardship. He endured the rebellion of sons and the disloyalty of trusted friends. Yet none of these incidents broke him. To the contrary, each served as a rung upon which he ascended higher until he became the living and enduring king of Israel. Each challenge and concealment of God's presence from him was transformative. (So it is with his people. Our Sages say, "Whoever is not treated to *hester panim* is not from Benei Yisrael."[8]) David treated each transformation as a *ḥanukkat habayit,* as a rededication of his spiritual structure. He greeted each with the song of *Mizmor Shir,* seeing himself as a new, revitalized being, ready to con-tinue propelling himself higher.

The *Beit Avraham* points out a few other curiosities. The first let-ters of the first three words of *Mizmor Shir Ḥanukkat HaBayit* coincide with the first letters of *mila, Shabbat,* and *ḥodesh* – the three practices specifically prohibited by the Syrian-Greeks. The first letters of the first four words spell out *simḥa,* "happiness." This is no coincidence.

The three practices share a single quality. They reinforce the bond and connection between a Jew and his Creator. Circumcision symbol-izes the quest for individual holiness, of curtailing and controlling our biological urges. Shabbat brings an individual and his Maker together, sharing quality time and closeness each week. Rosh Ḥodesh, the incor-poration of the waxing and waning of the moon into our calendar – symbolic of the irrepressible continuity of our people – is an expression of our dogged *emuna.*

The three work in concert with one another. Each element rein-forces the others and is reinforced by them. Holiness has direct bear-ing on *emuna.* Without keen and penetrating insight into the nature of Divinity, *emuna* is limited. But lack of holiness blocks our knowledge

---

8. Ḥagiga 5a.

of the divine. We cannot know Him without having something in common with Him. The more we are removed from holiness, the more we are removed from Him.

The reverse relationship is also true. Our progress toward holiness is largely determined by the depth of our *emuna*. The quality and intensity of our *emuna* enables us to take the difficult steps toward curbing our lower wants and desires.

Holiness and *emuna* both change and enhance the quality of our Shabbat experience. At the same time, when Shabbat is used properly, we draw from the light of Shabbat and make quantum jumps in our *emuna* and holiness.

Ḥanukka brings all these elements together, strengthening them and thereby increasing our *devekut* to God. Nothing brings us more joy than an unmistakable feeling of closeness to Him. This, perhaps, is why the Rambam[9] calls the days of Ḥanukka days of happiness.

---

9. *Mishneh Torah, Hilkhot Ḥanukka* 3:3.

Liberating the
Hidden Light

For all its beauty and profundity, when we study our Sages'
retelling of the Ḥanukka story, some of us want to do a reality check.
The miracle of the oil was important, to be sure, but why should it so
completely eclipse the military victory? Let us also not forget that if
not for that victory, there would be no rededication of the Temple
to speak of.

Moreover, our Sages have a very different take on the nature of
the problem that the Hasmoneans solved. We would (and do) point to
the terrible oppression by the Syrian-Greeks, their brutal suppression
of mitzvot and diabolical attempt to snuff out Yiddishkeit by banning
some of the pillars of practice. But this is not the way the Sages describe
the run-up to Ḥanukka. They note that the second verse of the Torah
uses four expressions of foreboding: *tohu, vohu, ḥoshekh, tehom*. Each,
they say,[1] alludes to one of the four successful attempts by an oppressor nation against the Jewish people. The Sages link the third, *ḥoshekh,*

Based on *Netivot Shalom*, Ḥanukka, 25–31.
1. Genesis Rabba 2:5.

or darkness, to the Ḥanukka period. Why? Because the Syrian-Greeks "darkened the eyes of Israel by telling them to write on the horn of an ox that they did not have a portion in the God of Israel." Is this the worst we can say about our persecution by the Syrian-Greeks?

Rashi[2] puts us on the trail of an important understanding about Ḥanukka. The Torah describes the lighting of the Menora immediately following the *parasha* of the offerings of the *nesi'im*, the princes of the tribes of Benei Yisrael, at the inauguration of the Tabernacle. Aharon, it seems, was dejected because he had no role in that event. The *nesi'im* had managed to walk away with every important contributory role. God reassured Aharon by pointing to his role in the lighting of the Menora, whose contribution would be greater than that of the *nesi'im*.

The Ramban questions why Aharon was appeased by this. Aharon certainly knew about the centrality of the priest to the *avoda*. In what way did lighting the Menora distinguish itself more than the burning of the incense each day or playing the crucial role in myriad offerings? Furthermore, a midrash[3] puts a slightly different spin on God's words of consolation. It has God telling Aharon that offerings – such as those brought by the *nesi'im* – are limited to the times that the Temple stands; the lighting of the Menora is forever. Is that really so? asks the Ramban. The Menora stood in the Temple. When the latter was destroyed, the lighting of the Menora ceased. What solace could Aharon have found in all of this?

The Ramban explains that God told Aharon about a special lighting that would take place well into the future. A family of priests – the descendants of Aharon – would wrest control of Jerusalem from the enemy and participate in the rededication of the Temple. This lighting, and the ones that would follow every year on the anniversary of the original, would not depend on the existence of the Temple.

God did not tell Aharon that He would compensate him in the future for not having a role in the inauguration of the Tabernacle. The midrash makes sense only if God responded to Aharon's concern with a role in the inauguration itself. His answer must be that the Ḥanukka

2. Num. 8:1.
3. Numbers Rabba 15:6.

lights are related to the Menora of the original Tabernacle, somehow extending their light even beyond the perimeters of the Tabernacle and the later Temples. The Ramban must mean that Aharon's descendants would take the Menora forward into time beyond its physical limitations. Alone among all the parts of the *avoda*, the lighting of the Menora would live on – not as a commemoration of things past, but as a continuation of the light of the actual Menora of the Temple.

The *Benei Yissaskhar*, citing the *Rokeaḥ*, finds an allusion to this in *Parashat Emor*. After visiting all the special days of the year – Shabbat and each of the holidays – the Torah switches topics[4] to the preparation of oil for the Menora. This also alludes to the unnamed holiday that makes use of that oil – Ḥanukka.

This is all so confusing. If the Ḥanukka lights represent a continuation of the light of the Menora , why are its halakhot so different? The Menora in the *Beit HaMikdash* was kindled during the day; not so the Ḥanukka lights. The Menora stood inside the Temple; we light the menora outside, at the entrance to our homes. The Menora required the purest of oils; the Ḥanukka lights do not.

The explanation begins with some difficult phraseology. "Toward the face of the Menora shall the seven lamps cast light."[5] Rashi takes "the face of the Menora" to mean the central lamp, which was not held atop a branch but rose from the trunk of the Menora itself. This is somewhat unsatisfying, though. Only six lamps turned toward the central one. Why does the Torah speak of seven lights turned toward the Menora's face?

We find an allusion here to the very nature of the Menora's light, whose source was the *or haganuz*, the original light of the first day of Creation. This was no ordinary light with conventional physical properties but the light of *Elokut*, Divinity. Too powerful for man to use, it was hidden away for some future time when man will be better prepared to utilize it. What we translate as the "face of the Menora," "*penei haMenora*," can be taken to mean the *penimiyut*, the inner essence of the Menora. That inner essence is the *Shekhina*, in the form of *bina*,

---

4. Lev. 24:2.
5. Num. 8:2.

shining through to the seven lower *sefirot*. The priest kindles the lamps and draws down some of this light from its source, illuminating our world with Divinity.

The Maharal explains the significance of the number eight. Seven (the number of days it took to create the world and all things in it, including the spirituality of Shabbat) sums up all things that are part of this world, including the spirituality inherent in it. Eight signifies what is beyond and above the natural. We circumcise on the eighth day, proclaiming the child's duty to add more holiness to the world than what is already there. The eighth day of the inauguration of the Tabernacle distinguished itself in ten different manners. We received the Torah on an eighth day of sorts – not the eight that is one more than seven, but the eight that is one more than seven squared, or the fiftieth day after the beginning of Passover. Despite the fact that the miraculous part of the oil's burning was that it burned seven days beyond its natural capacity, we celebrate Ḥanukka for eight days, in recognition of the nature of its special light and its lofty, transcendent plane.

In a word, that light can be identified with the continuation of the supernal light of the Menora, continuing to be available to us even in the absence of the Temple. This is what Ḥanukka is ultimately about: making that light available. Aharon was told that his descendants would inaugurate a holiday in which God would demonstrate that this light was a fixture of Jewish life. It would survive even the destruction of the Temple.

In a sense, there is nothing more precious to a Jew than that light. What could be more important than the light of Divinity that illuminates the Jewish soul? For that matter, what could be more devastating to a Jew than to be told that the light had been extinguished, that the *Shekhina* had permanently departed from the community? But that is precisely what the Syrian Greeks attempted to beat into the Jewish psyche – the sense that the *Shekhina* had abandoned them, plunging them into permanent spiritual darkness. The forced inscription on the horn of the ox says, in different words, that by sinning against God starting from the Golden Calf, the Jews had driven God away. He had now abandoned them entirely and left them to their own devices, devoid of any divine favor or illumination. No message could be more devastating to a Jew. It could have plunged them into a most frightening darkness.

It makes perfect sense, then, that we should mark the defeat of that plan through a holiday of illumination. How wonderful it is that we do so not by simply commemorating our past glory but by partially restoring it, through revitalizing the light of the Menora.

In truth, the light is available to us every Shabbat, but in a pristine form that requires our readiness to appreciate and receive it. Ḥanukka provides a different aspect of the light. Once a year, it would flare up with particular potency, illuminating even the darkness of the exile and people very distant from its source.

The events of Ḥanukka could not have happened at a more opportune time. They took place when Jewish spirituality was at its nadir, at a lower level even than at the time of the Purim story. From the time of the giving of the Torah, Benei Yisrael were used to an ongoing association with the Divine through the phenomenon of prophecy. Prophecy, however, came to an end just before the Ḥanukka era. The cessation of the sweet voice of divine communication plunged our people into darkness. (This is the reason that the details of Ḥanukka are not discussed in the Mishna and the holiday itself is mentioned only obliquely and in passing. Similarly, Ḥanukka is mentioned but once in all of the Zohar. Ḥanukka symbolizes a profound hiddenness, failing to emerge even in explicit words of Torah.)

The entire Menora was made from a single piece of gold,[6] from the bottom of its base to the ends of its branches and including all its decorations and embellishments. This is meant to teach us that the *or Elokut*, the light of Divinity, illuminates all spiritual levels, from lowest to highest. Although the *Shekhina* never descended below ten handbreadths, its light suffuses all places and levels. Similarly, Ḥanukka continues that illumination into the most inhospitable places and times of our exile. Our Sages fixed this holiday to light up our exile in the worst of times. Therefore, they deliberately placed the Ḥanukka lights within ten handbreadths of the ground – even though ordinarily the Divine Presence does not descend to within ten handbreadths – and outside our homes, casting its light on the entirety of the world, not just the inner sanctum.

---

6. Rashi on Ex. 25:31.

The Menora in the Temple required oil that was "pressed."[7] The *or Elokut* is generally incapable of entering and penetrating our coarse, unrefined natures. We must first "press" out the dross; only then will we yield the clear, refined oil within. We are required to negate our physical selves to God before we can contain His light. The oil we use each year on Ḥanukka, however, is not subject to any similar requirement. Part of Ḥanukka's specialness is its ability to reach all Jews at all levels. Ḥanukka is relevant to all of us, wherever we may be situated on our spiritual journeys.

We could not continue the long, arduous path of exile without it. It comes down to this: without the *or Elokut*, the Divine light, in our lives, we are nothing. With it, we can survive anything.

---

7. Lev. 24:2.

Shabbat Ḥanukka:
Getting It All Together

The motifs of Ḥanukka and Shabbat are so different that they seem to talk past one another. But every Ḥanukka has its Shabbat. When we probe more deeply, we will find that the two do not work at cross-purposes. Rather, they work synergistically to afford a unique opportunity for personal growth.

Detecting the apparent conflict is easy. On a number of levels, Ḥanukka and Shabbat aim at very different goals. Shabbat aims at more elevated precincts, while Ḥanukka concerns itself with more pedestrian ones.

Kabbalistically, Shabbat aims for the top of the list of the *sefirot*. The *Reishit Ḥokhma*[1] teaches that its light derives from the highest three *sefirot*; the *Be'er Mayim Ḥayim* explains that because of the ethereal origins of Shabbat's light, all impure forces melt in its presence. Ḥanukka, on the other hand, is assumed by kabbalistic literature to relate specifically to *hod*, the lowest of all the individual *sefirot* (if we take *yesod* and

---

Based on *Netivot Shalom*, Ḥanukka, 91–94.
1. *Shaar HaKedusha* 2.

malkhut to be collective ones). Shabbat and Ḥanukka, therefore, frame the opposite endpoints.

In our Shabbat *zemirot* we say, "Gladden them with *binyan shalem,* a complete structure;[2] make them shine in the light of Your countenance." Some see the "complete structure" in the sense of what we explained above. When Shabbat adds the rarified light of the three highest *sefirot* to what is ordinarily accessible from the other seven, the structure of the *sefirot* is fully potentiated.

We could suggest a different interpretation, one in which the tension between Shabbat and Ḥanukka is resolved. The "complete structure" is available specifically on Shabbat Ḥanukka, because Shabbat addresses the highest *sefirot* while Ḥanukka successfully takes God's light to much lower places. On the day that they overlap and fuse, all of the *sefirot* are addressed at once by God's light.

Our Sages imposed rigid requirements for the oils and wicks we may use for the mitzva of Shabbat lights. Those oils that do not produce a clean, constant flame or take well to the wick may not be used. They treated Shabbat Ḥanukka as an exception.[3] Even oils and wicks that do not burn well may be used. On one level, this reflects the halakhic reality that it is prohibited to make use of the Ḥanukka lights, and people will therefore not forget themselves and adjust a poorly burning flame, which would violate Shabbat prohibitions. At the same time, this halakha alludes to the idea of the "complete structure" of Shabbat Ḥanukka. Unlike other Shabbatot of the year, Shabbat Ḥanukka's reach and appeal are universal. Some people remain unmoved by the message of the ordinary Shabbat. Ḥanukka, however, casts its light to the nethermost realms, below ten handbreadths.[4] It attracts even those people who are like the imperfect oils and wicks, who are effectively banished from participating in an ordinary Shabbat, those to whom the light of Shabbat does not take well. These people respond to Ḥanukka and have a place at this one Shabbat that falls within it.

---

2. The direct reference is to the rebuilding of the Temple.
3. Shabbat 21a.
4. When a menora is placed at the outside door of a house, as it was in the time of the Gemara and as it is in Israel today, it is placed within ten handbreadths of the ground.

"How beautiful and how pleasant are you, O love, with delights."[5] Our Sages[6] see in this the beauty of a doorway framed with mitzvot. On the right is a mezuza and on the left, the Ḥanukka menora. If our approach is correct, there may be room in this image for another matched set as well: a house with a Shabbat candles illuminating the inside and set above ten handbreadths, while the outside is lit up by the menora, set below ten handbreadths.

This set is an inclusive one, because the implications of a menora that shines outside the house is that it acts as a beacon to those who find no place within the walls of holiness and the restrictions and limitations they involve. They, too, are part of the divine purpose for this holiday, just as the menora is set below ten handbreadths, recalling the spiritual poverty of the people at the time of the first Ḥanukka. God does not wish to see souls distanced and lost. Although generally the Divine Presence never descended below ten handbreadths, on Ḥanukka the *Shekhina* reaches out not only to the generally faithful but even to those who think they have bottomed out in their relationship with Jewish life.

The "complete structure" of Shabbat Ḥanukka incorporates as well the two poles in practical service of God. Some serve God primarily through an *avoda* that is upward reaching, above ten handbreadths. They serve God chiefly with their minds and hearts. Others direct their gaze to the ten handbreadths below. Acutely conscious of their lusts and desires, of where their evil inclination might take them, they busy themselves resisting its wiles and temptations and then taking the offensive to extirpate the evil entirely. There is beauty in both of these approaches, but what makes the structure complete is combining the two, of an *avoda* that leaves behind no part of man's own structure.

Indeed, the very names of the eponymous forefather of our people bear out the notion of the complete structure of man. On the one hand, he is called – like our nation as a whole – Yisrael. The word can be treated as an anagram for *li rosh*, to me is the quality of being the chief and head. But he never ceased being Yaakov as well, a name that derives from *akev*, the heel, or lowest part of the body. These names

---

5. Song. 7:7.
6. Soferim 20:5.

need not indicate a tension so much as defining the limits of the complete body of the Jewish people: serving God from top to bottom and losing nothing in between.

The Ten Commandments begin with what seems to be the ultimate reductionist statement of Jewish belief: "I am Hashem your God who took you out of Egypt." Seeing this verse as a simple call to belief in God, however, is a mistake. It is actually two calls. It sets forth two very different requirements of bedrock Jewish faith. It touches upon our core *emuna* regarding God as the Creator and continued Guide of all creation. But by linking "I am Hashem" – whom you know as the Creator – to our Exodus from Egypt, it evokes another key belief: the relationship of God with every individual Jew, owing to his being part of in the Jewish people. Not only did God forge us into a people, but He did so from within the context of an Egypt, where we had become mired in the impurity of the host culture and had fallen to the lowest of its levels. He could have insisted on beginning the process of growth and purification (which in fact occurred in the weeks before the giving of the Torah) while they still resided in Egypt. He didn't – to make the point that although we had little to show for ourselves spiritually, He was with us and took us as is.

These two aspects are combined and repeated each year on Shabbat Ḥanukka. Shabbat testifies to God as Creator. Ḥanukka demonstrates the relationship God has with His people, standing by them even when they have disappointed Him through their sins.

Shabbat Ḥanukka thus affords us an opportunity to experience the *binyan shalem*, the completed structure of the *tikkun* of all ten *sefirot*, of service of God with all parts of our being and *emuna* in both of its significant manifestations.

Purim and the
Four *Parashot*

Four That Are One

They are not well understood, but we have it on good authority that the four *parashot* we read in the period before Passover are laden with special potential: Rabbi Pinḥas Koritzer related that he achieved extraordinary episodes of *ruaḥ hakodesh* on these Shabbatot.

But why would reading another section of Torah text make a Shabbat essentially special? Why do we read these *parashot* at all? We note that they all grow out of mitzvot that can be fulfilled actively. Why read about them rather than just do them? If it is because we cannot fulfill some of them and wish to at least remember them, then why only these when there are many other examples? Why would the public reading of at least one of them – *Parashat Zakhor*, and possibly even *Parashat Para* – rise to the level of a Torah-mandated mitzva?

The common element to all of these *parashot* is that they support the all-important goal of *devekut*. Each *parasha* showcases a different factor in the long journey toward more meaningful connection with God. The message of each is so vital that it simply persists in all times, even when the mitzva with which it is paired cannot be practically implemented.

Based on *Netivot Shalom, Shemot*, 282–86.

Maḥatzit hashekel, the subject of *Parashat Shekalim,* the first of the four readings, connects a Jew to the Temple. The latter, and the offerings that were brought therein, point to the eternal bond between a Jew and his Creator. They address the sins that can tarnish the relationship between them and restore it to its previous luster. Each year brings a new cycle of offerings to the Temple; the half-shekel contribution of each Jew to the national fund for the purchase of communal offerings renews the commitment of a Jew to the service of the offerings.

The main idea behind the *avoda* is central and essential to us. It remains strong even in the absence of a Temple. Paraphrasing the Gemara[1], the Maggid of Kozhnitz taught that the Temple's destruction was restricted to its outer chambers. Its inner chambers were unscathed. The destruction did not and could not touch the place that hosts the primary bond between God and His people. (The Gemara[2] depicts the *Keruvim,* the golden cherubs atop the Ark, locked in an embrace at the time of the destruction, even though this was supposed to happen only at times when the Jewish people were faithful to their calling. The hour of the Temple's destruction, when divine wrath was vented on His House, would hardly seem to be such a time. The Gemara's point is that the connection between God and us remains even in such times. God engineered this manifestation of *devekut* precisely at the time of the destruction of the Temple to lend us comfort and support at such a difficult time.)

Amalek is the root and source of the *kelipa* (literally, "shell") of evil. The Torah speaks[3] of God placing His Hand upon His throne in an oath regarding the perpetual war with Amalek. The word for throne in Hebrew, *kiseh,* is spelled here deficiently, without the final *alef,* leading our Sages to remark that His very throne is incomplete as long as Amalek has not been eradicated. Moreover, no individual can achieve the full complement of *devekut* so long as Amalek's power is left unchecked.

While the mitzva of physically battling Amalek is limited to certain times and conditions and not applicable today, the inner meaning

---

1. Ḥagiga 5b.
2. Yoma 54b.
3. Ex. 17:16.

of the mitzva is very much with us. We address that inner core with a daily mitzva of remembering Amalek, and a yearly mitzva of doing so through the Torah reading of *Parashat Zakhor*. The contemporary mitzva demands of us that we do not make peace with the existence of evil for a single day – not within ourselves, and not in the world in general.

Parashat Para, the third reading, addresses a different dimension of evil. *Tuma*, spiritual impurity, is a related phenomenon, a state brought on by the existence and flourishing of evil. It is incompatible with *tahara*, its opposite. Thus, when man gives the *Sitra Aḥra* the opportunity to succeed, not only does he falter and fail, but impurity takes up residence within him. This impurity estranges him from God, moving him in the opposite direction of the *devekut* he seeks.

Without our Temple, we are unable today to deal with the layers and dimensions of spiritual impurity that used to be neutralized by the red heifer. The red heifer's ashes are central to the ritual of purification from halakhic impurity. Inner spiritual purity, however, remains an option through repentance and achieving *devekut* with God. Reading *Parashat Para* plays a role in this, as will be explained later on.

Parashat HaHodesh, the final reading, stresses the essential and central role of a Jewish court of law in determining when a holiday will arrive. All the spiritual gifts attendant to a holiday are dependent upon the deliberations of a human court. The heavenly court, as it were, operates in this regard at the behest of its human counterpart. The proclamation of the New Moon by flesh-and-blood judges sets off the cascade of spiritual reactions in the upper worlds that shape the content of the holiday.

The inner core of this, on the level of the individual, is the dependence of the *itaruta dele'eila* on the *itaruta deletata*. The *itaruta dele'eila*, the spiritual awakening from above, wherein God precipitates a response in man through some action of His, is dependent on the *itaruta deletata*, the awakening from below, where man precipitates a response in himself through his own initiative. All kinds of spiritual gifts are waiting to be sent to us from Heaven, but they require that we make something of a first move ourselves. Reading *Parashat HaHodesh* is such a move, whereby we draw down the holiness of the approaching holiday through an expression of the holiness already within us.

A well-established teaching of Kabbala sees every mitzva acting upon each of the four worlds: *atzilut, beria, yetzira,* and *asiya.* Those four worlds relate in the microcosm to four parts of our individual makeup: our bodies, and the three primary parts of our souls – *nefesh, ruaḥ,* and *neshama.*

Depending on our preparedness and intention, our mitzva performance takes place on different levels. Sometimes we perform a mitzva merely with our bodies. Sometimes, we function on the level of *ruaḥ,* or higher.

Without a Temple, it is impossible for us to perform many mitzvot according to their active, behavioral requirements. We must know, however, that these mitzvot have not disappeared or been shelved. The *neshama* of the mitzva still exists. They can be accessed through Torah. The Torah always functions as the cement between God and the Jewish people. When the *neshama* of a mitzva can no longer be joined to its physical counterpart in the *avoda* of the *Beit HaMikdash,* the substitute "location" for it is Torah itself.

Rabbi Moshe of Dolina explained why we recite the Torah verses dealing with the Exodus at the Passover Seder. The special light of the evening is resident within the words of Torah. By "doing" Torah – by reciting them – we gain access to that light. Similarly, we read the Torah section of *Vayekhulu* before Kiddush on Friday night in order to access the light of Shabbat that is resident in those verses.

We now understand why we designate a Torah reading for this particular group of mitzvot. Each is fundamentally important as a step toward *devekut,* and although their active fulfillment is somewhat distant and inaccessible to us after having lost the Temple, each remains realizable on the level of the *neshama* of the mitzva, even as its physical aspects are beyond our grasp. We enter into this level of observance specifically through words of Torah.

The Zohar calls Shabbat *yoma denishmata,* the *neshama* day. It makes perfect sense that Shabbat is the time best suited to engage these four pillars of our *avoda,* a realization that yields for us these four *parashot.*

Better Than Yom Kippur

It may be everyone's favorite Purim sound bite. If the tenth of Tishrei can be called *"yom ki-Purim,"*[1] then we feel a bit more reassured about how much pure enjoyment we anticipate on the fourteenth of Adar. For the comparison between the two days to hold, we need to understand just how Purim could be comparable to Yom Kippur. To the untrained eye, the two seem as different as apples and hamantaschen.

"Aharon shall bring atonement upon its horns once a year; from the blood of the *ḥattat* of atonement once a year shall he bring atonement upon it for your generations."[2] The two halves of the verse seem to mirror one another with a few key differences, such as that the first half stresses only "once a year" while the latter half refers to perpetuity. Commentators have written much about this verse, but we might propose a different approach than the ones they have taken. The verse alludes to Purim. While the formal atonement on the altar can only take place once a year on Yom Kippur, Purim provides a similar opportunity

---

Based on *Netivot Shalom*, Purim, 32–35.
1. Vowelized this way, the words mean "a day like Purim," rather than the day of atonement.
2. Ex. 30:10.

for atonement "for your generations," i.e., at all times, even when there is no Temple.

Purim and Yom Kippur are similar, but they are also quite different, and in some ways even opposites. They come from different places, as it were. Yom Kippur is deeply enmeshed in fear of God; Purim accomplishes its purpose through love. Atonement on Yom Kippur is for those who have engaged in repentance, but Purim atones even for those who have not, taught the Rebbe of Ruzhin. This, too, is a consequence of Purim's link to love rather than fear. (One opinion in the Gemara has it that Yom Kippur does atone without repentance. *Meor Einayim* explains this to mean that it affords atonement for some sins for which repentance is insufficient. According to this view, we should argue that Purim, then, brings atonement even for sins that Yom Kippur doesn't address.)

A comment of the Maharal leads us to another similarity – and difference. The Maharal points out that both Yom Kippur and Purim contain a resurrection theme. We tend to place resurrection of the dead at the end of history, as part of the final chapters of the book of humanity. Every Yom Kippur, however, is a kind of resurrection of the dead, in that people who may have been meted a death sentence while under divine scrutiny are given a new lease on life. In the Purim story, a Jewish people sentenced to death is brought back to life.

This very similarity, however, suggests the difference between the days. Resurrection of the dead is not of this world. It transcends nature. We would think that we have no role to play in such happenings, but we are taught otherwise. Even such a divine gift requires some human participation. Heavenly gates may open up to allow us access, but if we do not reach up and seize it, the gift does not help us. In more kabbalistic terms, any *itaruta dele'eila* demands that we respond to the gift and take hold of it.

Returning to what we stated before, if we view Yom Kippur as rooted in fear of God, we could paraphrase its essence as, "And therefore I will go in to the King." Purim, however, situated in love, has a different motto: "And thus I will go in to the King, although it is not proper that I do so."[3] Yom Kippur is preceded by a month and a half of intense

---

3. Est. 4:16.

self-examination and change, making it appropriate for us to approach Him. On Purim we enter before the King without any pretense of critical preparation, relying entirely on His loving embrace.

Yom Kippur's drama is higher profile. Everyone recognizes its holiness. Purim, explains the Ari, is so holy that its holiness cannot be recognized. It contains special elements that have no peer in Shabbat or any of the holidays. Its luster is so brilliant that it must be masked and disguised so that it can survive, unmolested by the *Sitra Aḥra*. The crown jewels, he said, make too attractive a target to move them openly from place to place. If they must be moved, they will be transported in a lowly wagon, mixed in with a load of rags. Their safety depends on appearing outwardly to be of less worth than their real value.

We do much of the same in some of our Purim practices. We don costumes, hiding our real identities; we drink in excess, acting as if we have no capacity to comprehend the deep significance of the day. The true nature of the day remains camouflaged and masked.

The *Torat Avot* contrasts the way Shabbat and the holidays work on our mood by citing an example of a king reaching out to a poor commoner. On Shabbat, the king brings the pauper into his palace, where he is mesmerized by his surroundings. He finds relief from his afflictions, because while he is in the palace he forgets about his commonplace existence. He is not so much happy[4] as stunned, dazzled, and intoxicated.

By contrast, on the holidays, the king takes up residence with the pauper in his lowly, simple home. This brings great joy to the pauper. Despite the limitations of his inelegant existence, he is able to host the king and enjoy his company.

We could add two more variations to this model. Yom Kippur is *Shabbat Shabbaton*,[5] or Shabbat taken to the next level. Here the pauper is taken not only to the palace but to the inner chambers of the king. The experience is elevating, overwhelming, and transformative – but it is not a time of happiness. Very different is Purim, where the king moves in with the pauper while his abode is not only simple but in disrepair and

---

4. And, unlike on the holidays, there is no halakhic requirement of happiness on Shabbat, only *oneg*.
5. Lev. 23:32.

disarray. The pauper's mood, darkened by his failures and his tribulations, turns to absolute elation through the king's visit. His joy is reflected in the eating, drinking, and rejoicing of Purim.

The example works well to describe the varied facets of our service of God. When we serve Him through learning and praying, using His tools, so to speak, we enter the King's palace. When we serve Him through the elements of ordinary life, by elevating our eating and drinking and other pedestrian affairs, we bring the King to our own homes. God created the world "in order to have a residence in the lower worlds";[6] raising up the ordinary is perfectly in sync with that goal. Purim, incorporating as it does much eating and drinking, presents a unique opportunity for elevating the ordinary. Purim creates the chance for us to pursue this noble goal even while we are mired in spiritual mediocrity. (This is yet another reason for our costumes on Purim. We remind ourselves that our shortcomings and faults are really superficial, like the costumes we wear. At our core, we are all loyal Jews possessing a divine soul from above.)

According to halakha, we give charitably on Purim to all who stretch out their hands to receive. We react to professed need with unstinting generosity, throwing to the winds our usual discretion about giving. Our teachers have taught us that this practice mirrors the pattern in heaven on Purim. There, too, all who stretch forth their hands from earth to receive are not turned away. On Purim, they tell us, we can merit providential solutions to our problems like no other day of the year. This, too, is part of the potency of the day – another way in which Purim shares power with Yom Kippur.

When we put this nature of the day to good use, we would be well advised to follow the example of Esther. Questioned by Aḥashverosh, "What is it that you ask … and what is your request?"[7] Esther's response instructs us how to present our own petitions on Purim. Given the opportunity to ask for anything, she says, "My life for my asking; my people for my request."[8] Now "asking" is the external manifestation of the inner "request," the latter being the core concern. Esther places her

6. *Tanḥuma, Naso* 16.
7. Est. 7:2.
8. Ibid. 7:4.

own life on the line with the word "asking." It is important, but it pales in comparison to the request, the value that is of utmost importance in her heart of hearts: the welfare of her people. When we probe what is central to our being and our focus on Purim, we come up with our commitment to each other as God's holy people.

On both Yom Kippur and Purim we are able to negate our own egos, interests, and selves, and see ourselves as part of God. Really, all the elements that these two days share flow from this commonality. The differences between the two holidays also flow from the different ways in which we achieve this *bittul*. We come to it through fear of God on Yom Kippur and love of God on Purim.

Light from within Concealment

They speak of Purim only in superlatives. Its holiness is unparalleled, they say; as discussed above, it equals that of Yom Kippur, the holiest day of the year. Its contribution to Tanakh – *Megillat Ester* – is claimed to be always contemporary. (Rabbi Baruch of Mezhibuzh explicates the mishna's instruction concerning the Megilla: "One who reads it *lemafre'a* – out of order – does not fulfill his obligation."[1] This means, he says, that if one reads it and believes that it applies to an earlier time period but not to the time of its recitation, he has botched the mitzva.)

As great as the day is, its special character remains elusive. We understand its message. But we know that each special day of the year conveys its own spiritual gift. That gift determines the day's *avoda* – what we must do to best receive that gift. What is it that we are supposed to take away from Purim?

Based on *Netivot Shalom*, Purim, 17–21.
1. Megilla 17a. The word connotes reverting to an earlier time.

In a word, the purpose of each of the holidays is that each person "should appear before Hashem."[2] Each of these days affords an opportunity to encounter God and be elevated thereby. Yom Kippur stands out among the biblical holidays. It is called *Shabbat Shabbaton,* or the chief Shabbat among the rest. The first Yom Kippur announced God's forgiveness of our sin of the Golden Calf, as well as replacing the first, broken set of tablets. We believe that the greatness of each special calendar day endures, and every year allows us to tap into its special theme and potential, propelling each of us to the greatest heights.

The rabbinically instituted holiday of Purim is the mirror image of Yom Kippur. If provides the equivalent opportunity for growth and advancement but from a diametrically opposite position. Purim takes our most depressed, spiritually impoverished state and allows us to turn it into greatness. According to the Gemara,[3] the Torah itself alludes to the Purim story through the words *haster astir,*[4] conveying the idea of hiddenness. In a word, Purim changes the elements of greatest divine hiddenness in our lives into spiritual elevation.

The Megilla is all about bottoming out. Its backdrop is a generation that in wholesale manner has given up on itself. The Jewish people had so little pride and self-esteem that they participated in Ahashverosh's meal, which celebrated his subjugation of them. The leaders of the people were so devoid of confidence and self-worth that every man – with the sole exception of Mordekhai – bowed and prostrated himself to the Jewish people's nemesis, Haman. Even Esther, when accepting the mission of intervention for her brothers and sisters, spoke in abject resignation: "And if I will be lost, I will be lost."[5] The doubling of the word "lost" enlarges its meaning to include body and soul together.

This state of affairs repeats itself often as periods of divine hiddenness that take hold of us as individuals or as a community. This, then, is the essence of our *avoda* on Purim – fully realizing the potential to find great elevation at times of spiritual doldrums. Because God's purpose,

---

2. Deut. 16:16.
3. Hullin 139b.
4. The letters of the latter word are close to those of "Esther."
5. Est. 4:16.

as it were, in creating the world was to find a suitable space for His presence in the lower worlds, the theme of Purim is eternal. The notion of creating greatness in a place of lowliness is inherent in creation. Purim, leading us from the abyss to the heights, is forever.

We cannot escape the conclusion that Purim has special relevance in our troubled times. We lost one-third of our people in the Holocaust, six million souls including the greater portion of our *tzaddikim* and *geonim*, through cruelty never seen before in our history as a people. This was followed by spiritual darkness that none could have predicted, whereby the evil inclination grasps even Torah scholars with two arms – on the one hand, a coolness in *emuna*, and the other, the heat of passion for evil lusts and desires. (The Jewish soul is sourced in the upper world of pleasure and therefore needs pleasure to thrive. When it cannot find permissible pleasures, it takes pleasure where it can, even from what is forbidden.)

The lives of many individuals also follow a predictable trajectory. So long as a Jew retains the fullness of his spirit, he is capable of enduring all suffering that comes his way. But when it is decreed from above that a person must endure the concealment of God's face from him, he is tested thereby with the spiritual suffering that comes from God appearing distant to him. Afflicted in this way in body and soul, a person comes to the conclusion that "it is because there is no God in my midst that all these evils have befallen me."[6] Inexorably, what follows is that God says, "I will *haster astir*, certainly hide My face on that day."[7]

These two factors taken together amount to Amalek's program. The numerical equivalent of Amalek is *safek*, doubt. When a Jew lives in the darkness of divine concealment, when he ceases to feel closeness to God, he begins to imagine a barrier between himself and God, and he starts to doubt the presence of God in our midst. This doubt plunges him into the clutches of Amalek, which brings the damping of his *emuna* as well as an explosion of his lusts.

How do we begin the climb from bleakness to elevation? The Megilla shows not only that it can be done but also how to do it.

---

6. Deut. 31:17.
7. Ibid. 31:18.

"Mordekhai cried a great and bitter cry."[8] Crying out to God is the beginning of redemption! Such a cry parts all the veils, smashes all the barriers between a person and his Creator. A cry that emanates from the soul of any Jew is more potent than all the forces of evil, stronger than the poison of Amalek and the designs of Haman. The cry may remain within, unheard by any person. It may come at a time that a person finds himself mired in defeat. (Consider the example of Esther. Our Sages tell us that when she entered the room in which Ahashverosh stored the royal idols, she sensed that the *Shekhina* suddenly bolted from her, and she felt utterly alone and vulnerable. She therefore called out, "My God! My God! Why have You abandoned me?")

Crying out to God is effective in all circumstances and at every level. It worked for our ancestors in Egypt; it worked for Moshe in defeating Amalek; it worked for Esther. Nothing stands in its path, although its effectiveness is linearly related to how great and bitter that cry happens to be. The potency of crying out to God for help against the depredations of Amalek is reflected in a number of Purim practices: the reading of *Parashat Zakhor* on the Shabbat before Purim, the reading about Amalek on Purim day, and the reading of the Megilla itself.

Crying out to God is effective as well against the Amalek that dwells within us. Beyond the cry that initiates the climb out of the depths, other Purim practices hint at measures that take us yet higher. The Megilla calls the days of Purim days of happiness. Indeed, happiness is both possible and important even to the person for whom concealment of the Divine has been decreed. A person can find satisfaction with the will of God and with the lot that is given him by that will, even when on the face of things that lot does not seem attractive. This is true of both material and spiritual aspects of his life.

Realizing that God remains present despite His concealment is fundamental to this happiness and joy. Our Sages allude to this when they tell us[9] that a person must read the Megilla at night and repeat it by day. The constant, dependable presence of God is with us always,

---

8. Est. 4:1.
9. Megilla 4a.

whether at times that His light shines through, or whether at times that it is concealed and we live in darkness.

(We do not mean to say that recognizing His presence in the darkness of night is the sole challenge. Reacting appropriately to His presence in the brightness of the day is also an *avoda*. The *Beit Avraham* tell us that Yaakov's reciting the *Shema*[10] at the precise moment that he was reunited with Yosef after so many years of longing and sadness was his way of taking his happiness and redirecting it to God. Similarly, when Mordekhai's plight was turned into triumph, and he was led through the city by Haman in a regal procession, he also recited the *Shema*. Here too he focused his joy on his relationship with God. He did not simply accept God's gift to him with thanks, but insisted upon immediately putting it to good use to cement his relationship with his Creator.)

Seeing the presence of God under all circumstances is ultimately the meaning of our Sages' directive[11] to us to drink on Purim until we do not know the difference between "blessed is Mordekhai" and "cursed is Haman." We must rejoice on Purim till we no longer feel the difference between the Mordekhai periods of our lives, when we merit insight and enlightenment, and the Haman periods, in which we find God's presence concealed.

The mitzvot of *mishloah manot* and gifts to the poor allude to a second measure we must take in pulling ourselves up from the depths. Our Sages direct us[12] not to be evil to ourselves in our own eyes. We can detect in this another meaning as well: Even if we believe ourselves to be evil, we should never allow ourselves to be alone. We have so much to gain by attaching ourselves to dear and loving friends. They can help us extricate ourselves from our failings, lifting us up from our lowly existence.

We show our commitment to others in two ways, representing two different levels of cherishing others. On one level, we value our friends, those who are close to us by choice. We evidence that friendship in the giving of *mishloah manot*. A higher level of appreciation of

---

10. Rashi on Gen. 46:29.
11. Megilla 7b.
12. Avot 2:13.

others is shown by our gifts to the poor. Through this we show our love for and commitment to the Jewish people as a whole, including those we do not know at all.

On either level, we will gain from our involvement with others. It should not be surprising, then, as we plod along in this period of *ikveta demeshiḥa* (literally, "the footsteps of the Messiah," referring to the times preceding the Messiah's arrival), when the concealment of God's light is greatest, that even our relationships with friends have become strained and difficult. The closeness between friends that was such an important part of even the recent past has been targeted by the evil inclination. Diminishing it is one more method of the evil inclination to plunge us into even greater darkness.

We are fortunate that the Holy One, blessed be He, provides us with the light of Purim once a year to turn the darkness of exile into light. We are also privileged that our Sages have mapped out for us the mitzvot that bring us to the unity we need in order to see it.

Passover

Shabbat HaGadol

I t is hard to imagine a Shabbat which is not great! What is it about the Shabbat before Passover that earns it the designation "the Great Shabbat," and the distinction of being, apparently, the greatest of the great?

The Gemara[1] tells us that we would be redeemed if our entire people observed two Shabbatot. This does not necessarily refer to two different weeks. Rather, the Gemara may be alluding to two separate and distinct aspects of a Shabbat well lived and appreciated. You can find a hint of the notion that Shabbat contains many facets in the Torah verse[2] "and observe My Shabbatot," in the plural. Shabbat contains a natural plurality; there are several ways to understand its different aspects.

Take the familiar set of *zakhor* and *shamor*.[3] At their root is the difference between the chief ways in which we serve God: through *ahava* and through *yira*, love and reverence. *Zakhor* instructs us to enhance

---

Based on *Netivot Shalom* 2:228–229.

1. Shabbat 113b.
2. Lev. 19:3.
3. "Remember" and "observe" – these two words introduce the mitzva of Shabbat in the two different versions of the Ten Commandments that appear in Exodus and Deuteronomy.

Shabbat through particular observances. Like all affirmative mitzvot, these are expressions of our love for God. *Shamor*, on the other hand, obligates us to protect the Shabbat by avoiding behavior that would be inconsistent with the day's innate holiness. When we rein ourselves in, when we obey laws that restrict our activity and keep us safe from the deterrents to a spiritual life, we serve God with reverence.

Two special Shabbatot hold positions of prominence on the calendar. One is *Shabbat HaGadol*, the topic of our discussion. The other is *Shabbat Shuva*, the Shabbat of Repentance, which falls between Rosh HaShana and Yom Kippur.

It is easy to see the link between these extraordinary Shabbatot and the dual nature of Shabbat we introduced above. Each of these special days relates to one of these two chief approaches to serving God. *Shabbat Shuva* focuses on our shortcomings in doing what God asks of us; it urges us to take our fear of God more seriously. *Shabbat HaGadol* opens a season of love between God and His people.

We know from the *Be'er Mayim Ḥayim*,[4] based on the Zohar, that all blessing flows from the Shabbat which precedes it. In a spiritual sense, whatever happens during the week began its journey toward us on the Shabbat before. The special gifts, then, of Passover and Yom Kippur are rooted in the Shabbat that precedes each of them. *Shabbat Shuva* joins us to the attribute of reverence, while *Shabbat HaGadol* binds us to our Creator with ropes of love.

Serving God with love is a loftier accomplishment, a more elevated state, than using reverence alone. While indeed all Shabbatot are great, two stand out because of the unusual bounty they bring us in advance of the coming week. Of the two, the one before Passover is the greater, because the attribute of love is superior to that of reverence.

Shabbat HaGadol, then, is truly "the Great Shabbat."

We can explore another approach. Shabbat invokes two distinct forms of *emuna*. By focusing on the events of Creation, of the necessary role of God in calling forth all phenomena as we know them, we affirm

---

4. Deut. 29:9.

out belief in God's existence. This view predominates in the first version of the Ten Commandments, as recorded in Exodus.[5]

The second version, however, shifts Shabbat's emphasis away from prehistoric antiquity to our beginnings as a people. We remember how a group of slaves was given safe passage out of Egypt as God unlocked the grip of a powerful enemy. We appreciate the distinctions God made in the process, deflecting the hardship and pain of each plague away from His people and directing it at the oppressor. In other words, Passover connects us with a more subtle kind of belief – belief in God's providence.

While one cannot possibly believe in providence without first accepting God's existence, it is certainly possible to believe in a God who does not choose to involve Himself with the details of human lives. Many non-Jews have deep religious conviction based on their belief in God. But God remains to them generally distant and remote. He can be reached through prayer, but He is felt as acting from a far-off place in heaven. We see God acting in a very different way – directly coordinating the smallest of events. We relate to Him as the One who "dwells on high, but lowers Himself to supervise both heaven and earth."[6] Our sense of the extent of His providence – of His constant involvement and immediate, local presence – creates a different bond, a more intense and immediate relationship.

Belief in providence, then, is the more sophisticated form of belief. Taken together with belief in His existence, we have the "two Shabbatot," the currency for acquiring our national redemption.

There is yet another avenue open to us. Shabbat goes by two different names. When first introduced in Genesis, it is simply called "the seventh day." This day contrasts an active period of creation, followed by God's cessation of activity and His introduction of rest. The world at large can respect and understand such ideas.

Only with the arrival and election of the Jewish people does the Torah attach a new label to this day and call it "Shabbat." Attached to the new name is the notion of *brit*, of a mutual covenant: "It will be a

---

5. Ex. 20:1–14.
6. Ps. 113:4.

sign forever between Myself and the children of Israel."[7] This Shabbat day, says the Torah, will be an eternal sign, an active and vibrant connection between God and His people.

This, too, is part of the "two Shabbatot" idea that leads to our redemption. It is rooted in the two reasons for Shabbat given by the two versions of the Ten Commandments: remembering Creation and remembering the Exodus. The notion of a seventh day, of a time of recognition of God's dominion, is inherent in the Creation story. The Exodus from Egypt allowed for another theme to be added. It turned us into a people, a nation that would forever share signs of closeness and bonding between ourselves and God.

Passover is also called "Shabbat,"[8] because it marks the time that we entered into a special relationship with God. The Shabbat that precedes the beginning of this holiday is the conjunction of two time periods that focus on this relationship. It is truly the greatest of Shabbatot – *Shabbat HaGadol*.

---

7. Ex. 31:17.
8. Lev. 23:12.

Searching for *Ḥametz*

Ask anyone who has readied a home for Passover. Getting rid of the spaghetti and chocolate éclairs is easy. The tough part is ferreting out *ḥametz* in its subtle forms: a trace contribution here, a product prepared in *ḥametz* utensils there. It takes focus and concentration to keep track of all the places *ḥametz* ghosts could be lurking. Hunting them down takes energy and perseverance.

This is precisely the way it is supposed to happen. A phrase straight from the Gemara[1] and *Shulḥan Arukh*[2] defines both what the law asks of us and how we can wrap our heads around the underlying concept. We are told to search for *ḥametz* even "in crevices and cracks."

Ḥametz, we are told, represents the evil impulse within us. The complex, laborious, time-consuming activities of searching for and destroying our *ḥametz* demonstrate to ourselves how meticulous we need to be in purging ourselves of our inner evil. We can begin by ridding ourselves of the obvious and apparent evils we harbor within, but we cannot end there. Evil is insidious. Like the invisible spores that waft

---

Based on *Netivot Shalom* 2:229–231.

1. Pesaḥim 8a.
2. *Oraḥ Ḥayim* 431:1.

through the air, settle on dough, and ferment it into *ḥametz*, a microscopic contaminant of evil can sour an entire personality. Nothing less than dogged persistence must be applied against the more subtle forms of evil within us.

We are even less inclined to act against evil that remains entirely undetected. Rabbi Menaḥem Mendel of Vitebsk's words[3] are telling. He cautions against feeling confident of a deep bond with God when we find ourselves transgression-free. Such a finding is meaningless. Perhaps, he argues, we have not sinned simply because the challenge hasn't presented itself. Or perhaps we remain untainted by a particular transgression because some external pressure, like embarrassment, prevents us from doing what we secretly would like to do, and not because we have harnessed or extirpated our evil impulses. It is quite possible, he says, that a person could live a righteous life, avoiding any activity that requires punishment, and yet learn that he failed in the chief task for which his *neshama* descended to earth – addressing some evil trait that lurked within.

This is what our Sages mean when they say[4] that *Biur Ḥametz*, the mitzva of ridding ourselves of *ḥametz* in our possession, requires *sereifa*, burning. In dealing with our active misdeeds, it is often enough to firmly resolve never to commit the sin again. Evil that has burrowed within us, however, must be cauterized and burnt out.

Tractate Pesaḥim opens with the words, "On the eve of the fourteenth, we search for *ḥametz*." Rabbi Ḥayim Vital reads this beyond its literal meaning. Having completed thirteen years since his birth, a young Jew stands on the threshold of responsible Jewish adulthood. Going into his fourteenth year, he must examine himself for any faults that prevent him from becoming a full Jew. When a Jew utters the blessing in the morning thanking God for not creating him as a non-Jew, he should ask himself if that blessing is fully merited. Is he the Jew he is supposed to be – thoroughly Jewish, without any admixture of foreign traits?

Similarly, as a Jew readies himself for the approaching holiday of Passover – the holiday that renews our peoplehood each year – he must

---

3. *Peri HaAretz, Ki Tissa*.
4. Pesaḥim 5b.

search for the internal *ḥametz* that blocks him from being the complete Jew that is his true role in life.

How can the search be effective when we are supposed to go beyond looking for the evil that we know about? How can we recognize the more insidious evil roots, when we often do not even know what we are looking for? Some of the answers emerge from the formal details of the law.

The mishna instructs us to search "by the light of a lamp." We might have preferred the brightness of daylight or the intensity of a large torch, but we turn down these options in favor of a simple, small lamp. *Ner*, the word for lamp, is spelled *nun resh*. These letters form an acronym for *neshama ruaḥ*, or the two components of the soul. If a person struggles as best he can to discover his primary root of evil, if he "searches as far as the hand can reach,"[5] his soul will take him the rest of the way and guide him to the truth. As the Slonimer adage goes, "The soul of a person will teach him." A Jewish soul contains much wisdom; it knows its origins and composition and can communicate back to its possessor.

Similarly, help comes from the Torah we have learned and mitzvot we have performed. The Zohar[6] comments on the verse "Or if he finds out that he has sinned":[7] "Who tells him? The Torah tells him!" The Zohar means that when a man's power of reasoning is insufficient to discover the source of evil within him, he can expect help beyond the limits of his own intellect. The Torah he has studied, the mitzvot he has performed, all leave an imprint on him. While a person may not feel their presence, He can rely upon them to light up the path of discovery. (This is alluded to in the mishna's instruction to search for *ḥametz* "by the light of a lamp," which resonates with "A mitzva is a lamp, and Torah is light."[8])

Other halakhic details fall into place. While most forbidden items become permissible when mixed in with a much larger quantity of

---

5. Pesaḥim 8a. The phrase describes the limit of responsibility in searching in hard-to-reach places.
6. Zohar 3:23b.
7. Lev. 4:23.
8. Prov. 6:23.

permitted material, *ḥametz* is different. The smallest amount of *ḥametz* contaminates a much larger mixture on Passover.

Evil corrupts. No amount of it can be tolerated or safely dealt with. The evil inclination acts like rot. The smallest quantity can infect healthy material and spread its disease. Like gangrene to the body, it must be stopped or it will take over.

We also understand, in a different way than we did above, why according to one opinion *ḥametz* must be eliminated specifically by burning it. The *Torat Avot* offers an analogy. Imagine a person who must clear a large stand of trees. Laboriously, his axe fells them, one at a time. After a while, he realizes that he can never complete the job in his lifetime.

He has another option. A controlled burn can clear a huge tract in a small amount of time. He can light a large fire that can burn all the unwanted trees in one vast conflagration.

Often, a person will take stock of his personality, resolved to clear out the dross. He will introspect and examine the quality of his actions and discover many things that are not right. He will search the "crevices and cracks" to get to the roots of his problems, calling upon the assistance of his soul and his Torah and mitzvot to enlarge his vision. When he completes this job, he will feel helpless. Each fault, each shortcoming, requires so much time! It will be impossible, he tells himself, to complete the job in several lifetimes.

What he must do is light a large flame. He must find a holy fire of passion and love for God. In one fell swoop, he will be able to accomplish what he cannot do one by one. He will be able to begin the holy festival of Passover in elevated holiness and purity.

Eternal Skipping

Why "Passover"? Why has this name, taken from God's "passing over" the Jewish houses, won out over all competitors?

There are so many themes associated with the holiday. The Torah itself frequently calls it the Festival of Matzot, while sometimes calling it the Festival of Spring. So many people think of it as a holiday of freedom. To be sure, we recall that God "passed over" the houses of the Jews while killing the Egyptian firstborn. It is hard to see, though, why this image is so much more striking and enduring than all others. Why did it stamp its imprint so thoroughly and confer the popular name on the holiday for all time?

The answer must be that passing over and skipping are the most essential and fundamental characteristics of Passover. Indeed, without some all-important passing over, there never would have been an Exodus.

Redemption is only secondarily about visible chains and shackles. Chiefly, it is about the inner nature of man. Man is redeemed when all the forces that keep him small, narrow, limited, and constrained are removed. Most of those work within him and are harder to break than the restraints of the taskmaster.

Based on *Netivot Shalom* 2:240–245.

Man can be redeemed only through awareness and enlightenment. The Egyptian experience, explains the Ari, was so steeped in the darkness of impurity that the *ḥitzonim*, the forces that encase holiness and obscure its light and purpose, had seized hold of *daat* itself. Man's understanding was compromised at its root. He was not simply challenged by conflicting claims to truth. His ability to discern truth was fundamentally impaired. Repairing the ravages of impurity never takes place in an instant. Man must always take small, incremental steps, raising himself arduously from one level to the next. He climbs higher one step at a time, and no steps can be missed.

Glimpses into the nature of God, in turn, also follow a distinct order. They do not come as disconnected impressions, arriving willy-nilly to one who seeks God. Deeper comprehension of God follows the order of the *sefirot*. Each *sefira* is a different tool, a prism which refracts the light of God in a different manner. Each makes its contribution but must be taken up in the proper order.

By all ordinary measures, whether looking at where man was or at the road the divine light had to take, redemption for the generation of the Exodus should have been impossible at that time and place.

God, however, specializes in accomplishing the impossible. By its nature, impurity functions only in places that are hidden from the clear, manifest illumination of His presence. He brought the redemption by causing such illumination of His light that the beclouding forces of impurity vanished in its presence.

On the verse in Song of Songs[1] "He [God] skips over the mountains," a midrash[2] sees an allusion to a dialogue between Moshe and the enslaved Jews.

Moshe: "In this month, you will be redeemed!"

Jews: "How can we be redeemed? Egypt is full of the ugliness of our idolatry!"

---

1. Song. 2:8.
2. Song of Songs Rabba 2 s.v. (2) *medaleg*

Moshe: "Because He wishes to redeem you, He pays no attention to your idolatry, but 'skips over the mountains.'"

The sense of this is that God revealed the extent of His love for the Jewish people by skipping! God's attribute of love was ignited through *itaruta dele'eila*, manifesting itself in great love for His people. (When God says, "I will lift you on eagles' wings,[3]" it means precisely His revelation of His great love for the Jewish people. He revealed this in His early proclamation calling them "My firstborn son,"[4] i.e., My cherished son.)

This revelation of love for the Jews from above was met below by a love for God that welled up in the Jews. With mutual love in place, the previous indiscretions of the Jewish people lost their significance. "Love covers all offenses."[5] Moshe's answer to the frustration of the Jews was that their idolatry would be washed away in the reciprocity of divine love.

This, too, required skipping and passing over. The Zohar[6] calls reverence for God "the primary commandment" and love of God, which can only follow in its wake, the second. When a person still mired in lowliness attempts to utilize love in his service of God, he runs the risk of attaching that love to inappropriate objects. To use love properly, his lower impulses must first be purified and elevated through the correctives of reverence for God. Only then can he make proper and satisfactory use of love in elevating his personality and enhancing his relationship with his Creator.

We see now why the word "Passover" is so fundamental to the holiday. No word could better characterize the deeper meaning and significance of the miracle behind the miracles. God smashed the Egyptian deities and tore asunder the laws of nature but not before He had violated rules even more basic. To redeem the Jews, God redrew for the moment the road map of human service to God and disturbed the rhythm of the *sefirot* by sounding an unexpected note. In both areas, He passed over all that was expected of man and of Himself.

---

3. Ex. 19:4.
4. Ex. 4:22.
5. Prov. 10:12.
6. Introduction 11b.

The poet wrote, "You lifted up Passover to the head of all the festivals."[7] With but a single exception, all festivals arouse divine love for Israel by first stimulating *itaruta deletata.* Passover, however, is the head, the source of all these festivals. The *itaruta dele'eila* of the original Passover not only made the Exodus possible, but it continuously nurtures man's quest for connection whenever he reaches toward God. To this day – in all places and under all conditions – when we inspire and arouse ourselves to closeness with God, we are in fact drawing from the great, holy love that God aroused within Himself at the first Passover.

Shabbat, too, is a consequence of *itaruta dele'eila.* As "an eternal sign between Me and the children of Israel,"[8] Shabbat arouses the great love God has for Israel, and through it, the love Israel has for God. Love, as we have seen, banishes all remembrance of wrongdoing. It is in this sense that we can appreciate the Sages' contention that "he who observes Shabbat is forgiven, even if he served idolatrously like the generation of Enosh."[9]

A widespread custom also points to the sharing of this theme of the display of divine love. On two occasions we recite Song of Songs, the perfect expression of the love between Israel and God and between God and Israel. The night of Passover is one of them. The other, not unexpectedly, is Friday afternoon, just before Shabbat is ushered in.

The power of redemption revisits us each year at Passover. "This night is safeguarded by Hashem for all of Israel for all generations."[10] In all times, for all Jews, in all situations and conditions in which they find themselves, redemption beckons anew on Passover and reveals the great love God has for us. Through the holiday of Passover, a Jew can tap into that love and draw redemption upon himself, freeing himself from his own personal limits and blockages. He can, if he wishes, extricate himself from any and all of the forty-nine levels of impurity and degradation.

---

7. R. Elazar HaKalir, in the *piyut* of the Haggada, "*Ve'amartem zevaḥ Pesaḥ.*"
8. Ex. 31:17.
9. Shabbat 118b.
10. Ex. 12:42.

We can explain in this manner the mystifying introduction to the Haggada: "*Ha laḥma anya*," "This is the bread of poverty." Generally, man's actions have a precise and measured impact upon the hidden spiritual worlds. Our mitzvot, our good deeds, our prayers create new patterns and combinations of the elevated spiritual forces. In a sense, we earn our keep, we help sustain the universe, we support its existence and well-being through our spiritual productivity.

Passover is different. Like the poor man begging for food, we receive something without paying our way. We were redeemed in Egypt despite lacking the spiritual currency with which we are usually expected to compensate God for what we take. Each Passover provides us as well with the same gift-basket of divine awakening, undeserved and unearned. We therefore announce, "All who are hungry, all who need, let them come." We invite all those who find themselves spiritually needy and wanting to partake of God's offer. It is a rare opportunity for us to skip over the usual plodding steps we usually need to take. We can avail ourselves of His great light, even if we are not deserving of it.

We are by no means finished uncovering what the name Passover teaches us about the fundamental character of the festival. The *Kedushat Levi* finds a remarkable clue in the difference between the names assigned by God and by *Klal Yisrael*.

God calls attention to the matzot, while we refer to the *pesaḥ*, the skipping over. Each emphasizes the love and appreciation that one party in the relationship has for the other. To God, the matzot represent the willingness of the Jews to follow His lead to an unknown and inhospitable wilderness, without thought of the next meal for themselves or their children. The speed with which they sallied forth into the unknown speaks eloquently in praise of their faith, trust, and love for their Creator.

The perspective of the Jews, of course, was quite different. They would point in awe at God's incredible sign of His love for them. The skipping over the Jewish homes during the plague of the firstborn displayed a divine providence and concern that was aimed at each individual. The Jews were not only saved down to the last individual, but their redemption was custom-tailored and micromanaged. How appreciative they were of the love and concern that accompanied this all-important and final plague.

Mutual admiration creates successful relationships. Taken together, the two names of Passover – including the cognomen that *Klal Yisrael* substitutes for the earlier, Torah-given one – tell one of the most important stories about the nature of the festival. God wished to create His people through the Exodus, but insisted on forging a relationship based on mutual love. We had to choose God as much as He chose us.

Here we discover another sense of the notion that Passover stands at the head of all the festivals. The reciprocity of love between God and His people expressed by the names of Passover defines not only a single holiday, but lays the foundation for the practice of the others. "You chose us from all the nations. You loved us, and were satisfied with us. You called Your great and holy name upon us.... Give us, Hashem our God, this holiday with love and willingness"[11] is an oft-repeated refrain of the holiday prayers. It accentuates our most important goal of the holidays: to implant, deepen, and nurture within us the feeling that God has chosen us.

This, too, is what we seek with the mitzva of *simḥat Yom Tov*, the holiday rejoicing and celebration. Through the holiday joy we declare that we are completely satisfied with God's conduct of our individual lives. (The Apter Rebbe used to stress that creation is fulfilled in a Jew's feeling complete satisfaction and joy in the way God conducts his life.) When we are pained and troubled with the vicissitudes of everyday events, our natural feelings are deadened or masked. We lose sight of our basic satisfaction with God's ways, frustrating our ability to feel our natural joy in our relationship with Him. Through the holiday celebration and the opportunity for peaceful contemplation of our lot with a settled mind, we remind ourselves of the essential joy that owes to being close to God.

---

11. From the holiday *Amida* prayer.

Expanding the Retelling

W hy is this mitzva different from all other mitzvot? "Whoever expands his relating of the story of the Exodus is praiseworthy," our Sages tell us, effectively urging us to act differently than in regard to other commandments. Ordinarily, we are not told to do more of a mitzva we have already fulfilled. Once we have taken the lulav, or heard the shofar, or even eaten the required amount of matza on the night of Passover, we are not urged to repeat the performance. Why is the mitzva of telling of the Exodus from Egypt different? Why are we told that we should preferably keep at it, even after we have fulfilled the minimum requirement?

Moreover, the mitzva of recalling the Exodus has a daily component. We fulfill it simply by our recitation of the *Shema*. We are not instructed to go the extra mile and lavish more time on this recitation. But we treat the parallel mitzva on the Seder night quite differently.

The Rambam[1] describes our obligation of telling of the Exodus from Egypt at the Seder. He has us fine-tuning what we speak about, according to each son's ability to grasp and digest the information. We include even the dullest of children – even the one who asks us no

---

Based on *Netivot Shalom* 2:247–249.

1. *Ḥametz UMatza* 7:2.

questions at all. We point to some servant and tell the child that we once served similarly until God took us out to freedom. We have more to say to the bright, mature son, relating to him the details of the many miracles that were performed through Moshe. The Rambam implies that there are no exceptions, that the father is required to instruct his son even if the son knows more than he! What point can there be to telling the son what he already knows, what he has listened to and processed in previous years?

In answering these questions, we discover the very essence of the Seder evening. Passover, simply put, is the holiday of *emuna*, belief. The Seder night acts as a Rosh HaShana in regard to our core belief in God. We recount the Exodus story on this night each year in order to implant and strengthen our belief. To help us implement this, the Torah created a special, elevated potency within our retelling of these events on the first night of Passover, which widens and deepens the quality of our belief. Each father relates to his son that which he heard from his own father, and he from yet earlier generations. Through this, they become united with all generations before, going back to the generation that left Egypt. This process has a remarkable ability to bolster and strengthen our belief, particularly at the time that "matza and *maror* are placed before you." Even should the son know more than the father, he stands to gain, because the specialness of the evening invests extraordinary power in the conversation between father and child. As the *Ohev Yisrael* put it, "On this night, the light of understanding of truth and belief is revealed. It hovers around each Jew. When a father tells the story, his words penetrate the heart of the son, and he is able to absorb their meaning and believe with all his heart."

We have a tradition that God Himself "observes," in a manner of speaking, the entire Torah. When the son asks his question, he is really asking our Father to fulfill the mitzva Himself, for Him to tell all of us the story in a way that we will more fully comprehend. We ask that God raise our belief consciousness to such a degree that it will spill over to all other days of the year.

With this understanding in place, we readily comprehend why we spend as much time as possible on this mitzva. At the core of the Seder night is the element of *emuna*, and there is no limit to *emuna*. Unlike other mitzvot, there is no set amount or quantity of *emuna* that once achieved fulfills our obligation. We always strive for more. Through the experience of the first night of Passover, in those few precious hours at the Seder, we can mine as much belief as we are willing to carry away. The more we take advantage of this special capacity, the more praiseworthy we are.

The Baal Shem Tov was once told from heaven that the Seder of a simple, ignorant villager equaled his own. The Baal Shem Tov sought out this commoner and asked him how he conducted his Seder. The villager admitted that he had no idea how a person was supposed to conduct himself. Lacking the knowledge, he substituted his own invention. Upon returning from synagogue, he would become very animated and excited and tell his waiting family about this accursed fellow Pharaoh. He would remind them that Pharaoh inflicted all kinds of troubles upon us and that God helped us and rescued us. "Come," he would say, "let us give thanks to Hashem, and drink a cup of wine in recognition." Having downed one cup, he would repeat his vituperation of Pharaoh and his thanks to God. In great agitation, he would renew the invitation. "Come, let us drink yet another cup in His honor!" This went on for several more rounds. There was nothing profound or insightful about his presentation. Yet his strong and unequivocal *emuna*, accompanied by passion and enthusiasm, left a great impression in heaven. His observance was so beautiful because the Seder's promise is realized in the clarity of *emuna*.

There are several other dimensions to the mitzva of telling of the Exodus from Egypt. We find no parallel in any other holiday, nor in any of the other great miracles that we experienced, such as the manna, or the well, which provided the Benei Yisrael with water throughout their many years in the wilderness. The Torah makes no demand that we gather our families and tell them the stories of other holidays and other miracles, even though they could surely contribute to a deeper and more mature belief.

Know this well. We completely lack what others call "commemoration." We never tell stories about the past, even about heavenly driven events which occurred but once in history. We are not interested in what has been, but in what will be.

The Exodus is important not for what happened in the early days of our peoplehood, but in what it brings us anew each year. Jews do not retell – they re-experience. The particular aspects of divine revelation that made the original Exodus possible are replayed and revisited upon us each year. The Maggid of Kozhnitz taught that each year, Jewish souls leave Egypt. The nature of the night is such that a Jew can escape the bonds (the *metzarim* in Hebrew) that restrain him and thereby win greater freedom. On this night a Jew can completely reverse his lot and escape all things that oppress and limit him. God's redemptive powers are, in a manner of speaking, in full and glorious display.

They are ready to be put to work for us. It is up to us, however, to trigger their release. Rabbi Moshe Cordovero taught that the revelation of these lights hinges on our involvement with them. Precisely through the mitzva of retelling the Exodus story and all its miracles, we make these lights available. Other great events in Jewish history were accompanied by miracles important in their day, but those miracles did not leave us with detailed narratives in which the lights of those holidays are embedded. Relating their stories in a fixed manner, therefore, is not the key part of the holiday.

The Haggada's author instructed, "In every generation a person must regard himself as if he left Egypt, as it is written,[2] 'Because of this, Hashem did all of this *for me* as He took me out of Egypt.' He redeemed not only our ancestors, but us as well." This is literally true. Because of the eternal redemptive character of Passover, we can all become redeemed anew at the Seder. We are as much included in this divine gift as the generation that walked out of Egypt. Here we discover another reason to go the distance in retelling the story. Our Exodus conversation is the currency with which we pay for this divine illumination. When we offer more, we are given more.

The Zohar tells us that speech itself was exiled in Egypt. While in bondage, the Jews did not have the ability to communicate properly. They could not express themselves properly to God. (This explains Moshe's oft-repeated refrain that he was of "uncircumcised lips"[3] or "not

---

2. Ex. 13:8.
3. Ex. 6:12.

a man of words."[4] As the leader and representative of his people, their limitations became his. Their constricted power of speech manifested itself in Moshe as well.)

Initially, in fact, the Jews' power of speech was so hampered that they could not even manage preverbal speech – vague thoughts not even formulated in words. "With the passage of many days, the king of Egypt died. The Jews groaned from their labor and cried out to God."[5] This should be understood as a change for the better, as the beginning of their redemption. Prior to this, they could not even groan! As the redemption approached, they were given at least this much ability, although more expressive speech would have to wait before its shackles would be loosened.

With the Exodus from Egypt, speech emerged from its captivity. It is fitting that we exceed the minimum in retelling the Exodus story, because the Seder night marks the triumph and redemption of the power of speech itself.

---

4. Ibid. 4:10.
5. Ibid. 2:23.

Four Hasidic Sons

Barukh HaMakom; barukh Hu. This short paragraph in the Haggada uses the word *barukh*, blessed, four times, one for each of the four sons in the section that follows it. This is indeed the point. The evening holds out a promise to all, in whatever spiritual circumstances they find themselves. The most important encouragement we can receive is the knowledge that God treats each Jew as a son. Each one of them owes God a special and different blessing of gratitude. On the night of Passover, no one is left behind.

The wise son notes the myriad halakhic details of the Seder evening. "How is it that all the halakhic nuance – the mitzvot that take the form of remembrances and statutes and laws – seems to work so perfectly for you, and fails for me? Through the mitzvot of Passover you have merited closeness to God. I have tried the same. I have been faithful to the same details in the law, but I have not attained this *devekut*. Where have I gone wrong? What is your secret?"

We answer with a point of law about the eating of the Passover offering: it comes at the very end of our meal. We eat nothing afterward; we eat it at the point that we have sated ourselves, and our stomachs

Based on *Netivot Shalom* 2:253–255.

do not call out for more. In a manner of speaking, we put our ordinary food concerns behind us before we are ready to approach the central mitzva of the evening, the eating of the Paschal lamb.

Therein lies the difference between a mitzva performed and *devekut* achieved. You may be meticulous in your observance, we tell him, but you need to do more than that if you wish to live at the spiritual cutting edge. If you wish to know true closeness to God, if you choose to find your chief joy in bonding with Him, you must wean yourself away from the pursuit of earthly enjoyment. If you dull the experience of a mitzva by marrying it to less worthy pleasures, don't expect the ultimate spiritual payoff.

The evil son is not an incorrigible reprobate. He has not walked out of Jewish life. What makes him a *rasha*, an evildoer (in his own eyes) is harboring an active and vigorous evil inclination that allows him no peace. He sees himself falling for its blandishments more often than do his friends and associates.

Dejectedly, he approaches yet another holiday. He has been there before. He looks jealously at those around him, all eager and expectant, awaiting the privilege of participating in a great event. He has tried that all too many times. With each attempt to do the right thing, he is confronted by roadblocks of difficulty and temptation. He is convinced that he is a creature living apart from others. "Look here! The rest of you go about your mitzva observance undisturbed. God protects you from constant assault by the evil inclination. Proper *avodat Hashem* is therefore possible for you. It has no relevance to someone like me, beleaguered as I am by the evil inclination every time that I try to improve my spiritual state. With the fire of an aggressive evil inclination burning within me, my service of God amounts to nothing."

We tell him that had he been part of the generation of the Exodus, he would not have been redeemed. How different are you, we tell him, from those who lived back then? They had descended to the forty-ninth level of impurity. Do you believe yourself worse than them?

Yet they were redeemed, but you would not have been. They succeeded because they never despaired, never lost hope. They always believed that there would be a redemption because they saw themselves as redeemable. Sin will not keep a Jew from his Creator. Despair will. Despair, not your evil inclination, is your nemesis.

His despair may be a function of his personality. But it may also flow from a serious flaw in his thinking, one that is more problematic than the shortcomings in his actions. He may lack confidence in the specialness of the Jewish *neshama*. Doing so, he effectively denies one of the principles of faith, the mystical power and resilience of the Jewish soul. He deserves to have his teeth blunted; effectively, he embraces heresy. A Jew is obligated to believe that God chose us from all other peoples, and that He never abandons us. He continues to dwell among us in the midst of our impurity. This belief is crucial to any change for the better, to the possibility of redemption. Believing in it made the redemption possible for the generation that left Egypt; believing in it will be crucial for those privileged to witness the final redemption as well. Without it, our despairing friend could not possibly have been redeemed had he lived back then.

We can offer an alternative reading. The *Noam Elimelekh* teaches that there is a spiritual world called "the collective of Israel." This world is unblemished, because only individuals sin. The group, the larger entity, remains without fault. It therefore serves as a refuge for people who have fallen short of their expectations.

The evil son "removes himself from the collective." He asks, "Why do you perform the Seder mitzvot in these large gatherings? Why do you band together? Would it not be more dignified, indeed more fulfilling, for the individual to serve God in the privacy of his own surroundings and thoughts? Must I really join with others to do what I would prefer to accomplish on my own?"

You of all people, we tell him, would find that a dead end. The best way for a sinner to extricate himself from his past is to join with the many. You can still find a place in that world of the collective, even if you have not built up your own.

Hasidim say, "Do not be an evildoer by yourself."[1] If you are to be an evildoer, do not go it alone. Join with the collective; throw yourself into the group. In it, you can still find redemption.

The third son is simple, unencumbered. He presents no great enthusiasm or passion, nor any mockery or cynicism. Rather, he suffers

---

1. Eisenstein, *Otzar Midrashim*, 271. The idiomatic intent of the passage is: "Do not be evil in your own eyes."

from indifference. He is insensitive to, and uncaring about, the universe of *kedusha*.

What can we tell him that will make a difference? He is dead to the message. (*Tam*, or simple, is the reversal of the Hebrew letters for *met*, dead.) We can only offer this: "Hashem took us out with a strong hand."[2] You must do the same. You must rouse yourself from your torpor, shake off the lethargy. Only through your own strong hand can you push yourself out of your numb resignation and awaken forces of the soul that may be dormant but are surely there.

The fourth son is closed off. We see nothing entering, nothing leaving. His heart is closed, his mind is sealed. His entire essence, really, is shut off to any change or inspiration. He reacts to nothing and cannot even formulate a question.

We have no easy remedy for his difficult state. But we do have a collective memory. Our Sages liken the generation of the Exodus to a fetus in a womb. In other words, we were also sealed off, covered and encapsulated. We had no plan. We did, however, have simple faith. We believed that God would make things better.

This simple faith is the best – the only – option we can offer him. We tell him, "Because of this, Hashem performed for me when I left Egypt."[3] It worked for me. It will surely work for you. Push on; serve God even in your current state. But keep focused on your simple, core belief in God's existence. Somehow, it will work out.

There is, we discover, a common thread to the spiritual malaise of all the sons. None are beyond the pale. Each of them can use the holiday of Passover to transcend his troubles. Even the evil son can put his evil behind and become one of the enthusiastic participants.

Thus we tell him, "Had you been there, you would not have been redeemed." There, in the days before we received the Torah, your despair might have marginalized you, left you behind. But we are not there anymore. We have since received a Torah. The Torah writes off no one! The holiday of Passover offers a protocol for change, a road back paved with opportunity for anyone who wants to travel it.

---

2. Ex. 13:14.
3. Ibid. 13:8.

Begun in Shame

T wo opinions in the Gemara[1] dispute how it is done, but all agree about the essential premise. The mitzva of retelling the Exodus story on the night of Passover begins in the murkiness of ancient shame and only then proceeds to national triumph.

Rav instructs us to begin by mentioning the idolatry of our earliest ancestors. Shmuel moves up the shame to the period of our slavery in Egypt. Neither opinion strikes us intuitively as correct. Why should we not begin our account with the panoply of wonders which God performed for us in taking us out of Egypt? Would it not be more effective to launch into a description of how God made a mockery of the usual restrictions of natural law by His wholesale violation of them?

Come to think of it, why should we see our servitude as shameful? We were led into it by divine decree, but not because of some terrible transgression we had committed!

These questions strike us as significant only because we have accustomed ourselves to a mistaken notion about the mitzva of retelling

---

Based on *Netivot Shalom* 2:252–253.

1. Pesaḥim 116a.

the Exodus story. Many of us believe that we best perform the mitzva by focusing on the wondrous miracles that God performed for us. This is a mistake. The essence of the mitzva is relating how we became God's chosen people. It is therefore crucial that we begin with our shame, with the nadir of our ancient past. By emphasizing our lack of worth, we appreciate our election in a very different manner.

Because we were unworthy of being selected, His choice is all the more important – and all the more enduring. God chose us because His will dictated it. There was no cogent "reason" for Him to pick us. Will knows of no reason and needs no reason. It just is. He chose us as an expression of divine love, which flows from His inscrutable will. Had we been worthy, had there been some compelling reason to choose us, God's love for us would have been a contingent love. It might waver or vanish if that reason ever disappeared. Because we were selected without any reason justifying the choice, we can rely on the eternal continuity of His love.

It is because of this as well that God seems to have inappropriately called us "My firstborn son"[2] while we were still mired in the degradation of Egypt, when we had not yet done anything to deserve that distinction. Would it not have been more appropriate to wait until we had earned the title through our mitzvot before awarding it to us? Had He done so, however, our appointment would seem predicated on some achievement or sterling characteristic. God wished to make the point that our election was not contingent on anything.

There was indeed no shame in their forced labor in Egypt. The Jews had no control over the circumstances that led to their being pressed into service. A divine decree, foretold to Avraham, dictated the labor and the oppression. This is not the shame about which we speak.

The shame was in where the servitude had taken them. Prior to the Exodus, the Jewish spirit had been swallowed up entirely by the Egyptian beast. Jews had no sense of independent existence and identity. They had become slaves in spirit, not just in practice. This loss of self-worth was not part of the divine decree and was very much a source of shame. (This loss of personal significance is the real meaning

---

2. Ex. 4:23.

of the statement that they had become mired in the forty-ninth level of impurity.)

The Exodus changed this for all time. No subsequent oppressor would ever be able to completely subordinate them. While they might be successful in inflicting all kinds of harm upon them, from then on they would never be able to vanquish them in spirit.

This discussion sheds new light on the dispute between Rav and Shmuel that we mentioned above. The two do not simply choose between two large stains on the Jewish national record. They disagree about the defining attributes of the Jewish soul and essence.

To Rav, the most important element of being Jewish is belief in God. Understanding God and His oneness precedes all other considerations of Jewish life. Rejection of that belief – in a word, idolatry – is the polar opposite of what we are as Jews. There can be no greater shame, no more extreme departure from what is appropriate to us. We begin the story, says Rav, by recalling our roots in the idolatry of our ancestors.

Shmuel's reasoning dovetails neatly with our words before. The Egyptian servitude was not just an outrage to our freedom and dignity. It left us asphyxiated for Jewish air. It smothered and suffocated, denying us our own identity and imposing in its place a perverted Egyptian one. To Shmuel, what makes us fundamentally different from all other peoples is *kedusha*. There could be no greater Jewish shame than to be firmly and seemingly inextricably ensconced in its opposite, in the degradation of Egyptian culture. We begin, therefore, with "We were slaves to Pharaoh."

It is safe to say that between the two opinions, we have arrived at what it takes to be a Jew. *Emuna* and holiness are the twin foundational elements of Jewish life.

Probing deeper, we realize that the two are bound up with each other. *Emuna* is part of the fabric of the Jewish *neshama*. When we find ourselves plagued with questions, criticisms, and doubts about our belief, something has robbed us of our natural birthright, or the certainty resident in the Jewish soul. The culprit typically is a shortfall in holiness, which will dull the luster of the Jewish *neshama* and mute its primal call.

Happily, the opposite is also true. When we grow in holiness, we can expect greater clarity and brilliance in our *emuna*. Insights that evade us while our *neshamot* are coarse and unrefined become available to us when holiness adds refinement to our souls.

These two all-important elements of Judaism were addressed in the events just prior to the Exodus. We were instructed in two mitzvot, both of which involved blood. Smearing the blood of the Paschal lamb on our doorposts was a powerful demonstration of our belief in God. We not only accepted God's existence, but understood that His providence extends to all individuals and selects between the innocent and the guilty. We did not fear the expected reprisals by the incensed Egyptians.

The blood of circumcision showed that we were determined to pay a price to incorporate the values of holiness, starting with the curtailing of license and passion, which is a central theme of circumcision.

We can offer yet one more approach to our topic, one which takes the ignominy of our early history and stands it on its head.

Sophistication takes time. Complexity generally goes hand in hand with a longer process of development. No creature emerges less complete and more dependent upon others for care than humans. A one-day-old baby is no competition for a foal of the equivalent age. It takes far longer to become half an adult human than half a horse.

Inanimate objects, on the other hand, inherently possess all the qualities we find useful and interesting. We never wait for them to grow up or mature. It seems to be a rule that those who arrive at the top of the developmental ladder of nature begin as slow starters.

So it is within human civilization. The Jewish people, destined to achieve the best that God had in store for the human race, would also have to undergo a slow development. Their humble, faulty beginnings actually point to their great potential. Their transformation can now be understood as part of the global rule concerning growth and development. What the Jews would ultimately possess spiritually was so important and deep that none of it was present during the infancy of our people.

Their beginning in shame turns out not to be so shameful at all.

The Plague of the Firstborn

The Exodus broke not only the shackles of slavery of the ancient Benei Yisrael, but overcame the power of evil that truly subjugated them. The infamous impurity of Egypt was subjugated, allowing a people to reunite with the spiritual legacy of the forefathers. We believe that this triumph of good over essential evil had consequences not only for that moment but for all time.

This did not happen in one instant. The Ari explains that evil was reduced stepwise, retracing the stages by which the will of God was transformed through the *sefirot* until it reached us as concrete reality. Each of the *sefirot* is opposed by a countervailing force. To make room for holiness, these anti-*sefirot* were serially destroyed; each of the ten plagues shattered one of these repressive forces.

Traditionally, we differentiate between the lower seven *sefirot* and the upper three. The first seven correspond to the days of the week, or to the sum of all physical activity, and each has a corollary in the system of evil. Each negative *sefira* was unseated through one of the first seven plagues.

Based on *Netivot Shalom* 2:263–267.

The upper three *sefirot* are the holiest. They lie beyond our immediate grasp and are not related to physical manifestations.[1] Their counterparts in evil are the most pernicious. Only the shining of a much greater light from the upper *sefirot* could counteract their effect and subdue them. This is precisely what happened in the last three plagues, culminating in the final plague, which dealt the death blow to the intense darkness of the corresponding negative *sefira* of the *Sitra Ahra*.

(We witness a related phenomenon each week. The kabbalistic works stress that "all the dominion of harshness and the forces of judgment[2] flee" before the holiness of Shabbat. Shabbat is accompanied by illumination from the upper *sefirot*, and evil cannot coexist with that light.)

We now discover the fuller meaning of God's promise that "I will bring to judgment all the gods of Egypt."[3] This verse explains why God Himself – meaning no angel or messenger – would pass through Egypt visiting the plague of the firstborn upon the Egyptians. In order to bring the Egyptian gods to judgment, i.e., to crush and neutralize all the forces of impurity, nothing less than His presence would suffice.

Unlike any of the preceding plagues, the Jews required some sort of identifying mark distinguishing them from the Egyptians to weather the effects of the plague of the firstborn. The forces of the *Sitra Ahra* always rise in opposition to the display of anything good and holy. Their amplified presence would imperil anything lacking special protection. Thus, the Jews required the blood of the Passover offering on their doorposts. Such protection was not needed during any of the earlier plagues, when the evil forces would not operate on as feverish a level.

---

1. These three *sefirot* are sometimes called *mohin*, or intellects. While the first seven are accessed by us through the discrete physical activity of the mitzva system, we tap into the upper three primarily through intellectual output and understanding. Indeed, the names of these *sefirot* correspond, for the most part, to intellectual processes.
2. In other words, what we refer to as evil. All evil phenomena stem from the exactitude of God's attribute of judgment, which can mask the effects of the more essential and primary attribute of God's compassion.
3. Ex. 12:12.

Had all gone according to divine plan, had the Jews followed the divine lead more perfectly, the Exodus would have been the beginning of the final and complete *tikkun*. The Exodus would have led directly to the closing acts in the drama of human growth. In retrospect, the Jews were sent to Egypt for this very mission. They were meant to stare down the full display of evil that was resident there, and endure, survive, and triumph over it. Their triumph was to break the back of the oppressive force of evil and change the way man would relate to it. The weight of evil would be lifted at its source and the *tikkun* could proceed. Because of our failings with the Golden Calf and other episodes, the complete *tikkun* is still something we are waiting for. But our mission was not a total failure; the power of the *Sitra Aḥra* remained blunted and curtailed.

In the immediate aftermath of the plague of the firstborn, the Jews emerged as a people. The breaking of the force of evil and the creation of a people chosen by God are not coincidentally related.

The Jews could not possibly become a special people so long as the darker forces reigned in their full strength. They had become, at the time, fully enmeshed and ensnared in the forty-ninth level of *tuma*. Spiritually, they could emerge from the more important inner captivity only after God revealed His presence so powerfully that evil was broken at the level of the anti-*sefira* related to the highest of the upper three *sefirot*, *keter*.

Our Sages[4] explain why Moshe told Pharaoh that he would pray to God to end the plague of hail only after he left the city. Moshe refused to pray within the precincts of an Egyptian city, which was contaminated by the presence of idols. It was not a place to seek the company of the Divine Presence. On the other hand, this same Divine Presence came to that city and to others to strike at the firstborn and overwhelm the forces of evil.

Here is the crucial point. Ordinarily, the *Shekhina* will not visit a contaminated place. The spiritual necessity of the Jewish people, however, trumped all other rules. For the good of His people, God will make an exception.

---

4. *Mekhilta, Bo* 1, cited by Rashi on Ex. 9:29.

The laws of Ḥanukka, interestingly, offer a parallel. The *Meor Ein-ayim* puzzles over the law that optimally positions the menora within ten handbreadths of the ground. The *Shekhina*, according to our Sages, never descends to within ten handbreadths of the ground. Why do we prefer placing the menora in an area that the *Shekhina* regards as off-limits?

The answer, he says, is that in order to rescue *Klal Yisrael*, the Divine Presence will sometimes reach out to places it usually avoids. Prior to the victory of the Hasmoneans, the Jews were spiritually far from where they should have been. They were, in a manner of speaking, below the ten-handbreadth line. Despite this spiritual infirmity, the Holy One, blessed be He, reached out to them in order to save them. We memorialize this deliverance in placing the menora in that low position.

We have now hit upon a second reason for God's direct involvement in the plague of the firstborn. Having loosened both the physical and spiritual bonds that had held the people, it still took God's manifesting breathtaking love to forge a compact between *Klal Yisrael* and Him. As the *Or HaḤayim* writes, God spurned the possibility of deputizing any angel and insisted on performing the final plague Himself, in order to evidence His love for His people. The newly freed Jews agreed to become His special people because of this extraordinary display of love.

The slaying of the firstborn exacted a "price" from the Jews. "All the first-born among the Jews have become Mine; on the day that I smote the Egyptian firstborn I made them holy for Myself."[5] This implies much more that an obligation to redeem a firstborn son from a priest. It underscores a most important principle in growing toward God.

Bekhor, which means firstborn, also means "choicest." Every think-ing Jew understands that by offering to God precisely what he holds most dear and cherished, he shatters the power of forces that come between him and his Creator. He freely offers to God every aspect of his existence that he finds to be firstborn, choice and beloved. He holds back nothing.

The laws of redeeming the firstborn allude to the fullness of this concept. We are instructed to redeem the first among our children,

---

5. Num. 8:17.

among our cattle, and among the donkeys. They symbolize different interests, all of which have to be properly removed from our sense of ownership and personal proprietorship and offered back to God. Some of them are uniquely human, reflecting the more elevated parts of our selves. They are represented by the firstborn of our offspring; we are told to consecrate that first child to God. Some are manifestations of our lower, animal nature. We therefore consecrate the firstborn of the cattle. Still others we can regard as debased even within the animal realm. The donkey represents debased animal life, or the life of sin. We strive to offer all of them to God, knowing that if we do not, the self-centeredness and self-indulgence that they breed creates distance between ourselves and our real Beloved. We redeem them by placing them before God with alacrity and announcing to Him, "See, we withhold nothing from You, not even that which we would otherwise treasure the most."

The firstborn donkey, representing what is illicit, cannot be consecrated in its own right. It cannot be devoted to God, elevated, and purified. As the Torah instructs, it must be broken. We cannot speak of elevation and holiness without first detaching ourselves from their opposites. For the loftier (or at least more redeemable) interest of our lives, there is a more noble course of action.

"All the firstborn among the Jews have become mine…I made them holy for Myself." Consecrating the firstborn is a prerequisite to becoming holy to God. The earliest stage in a Jew's service of God (beyond eschewing the evil and sinful) is elevating the firstborn – agreeing to offer the choicest he has to God. To begin with, he does this by extending the treatment of "firsts" to everything in life. Before he takes any pleasure from this world, his first encounter is through reciting a blessing. He takes time to think about what he is about to do and brings God consciousness to it. He reminds himself who his benefactor is, thereby binding himself to God before enjoying the food. This is the essence of the offering of the first fruits and the first grains. His enjoyment now knows a partner – he has invited in God to the experience.

This is only the beginning. And it applies specifically to things and experiences that are not otherwise forbidden. He will go on to greater achievement, as God becomes a larger part of the partnership.

The *Mesillat Yesharim*[6] explains the difference between *tahara*, purity, and *kedusha*, holiness. The former involves abandoning the negative, jettisoning the evil even within what is technically permitted. The latter turns everything – even pedestrian events like eating and drinking – into holiness, akin to partaking of offerings in the Temple. We get to the first level substantially on our own power. Having done whatever we are able to do, we are boosted to the next by a gift from Heaven.

Look once more at the verse with which we began this section, and you will see how far along the Jews were transported at the time of the Exodus. First, they witnessed the destruction of every "negative firstborn" – every value and interest in Egyptian society that was mired in immorality or completely without redeeming value. They resisted the depraved values of the Egyptians and pledged their allegiance to higher values through the blood of circumcision and the blood of the Passover offering. Their performance of these mitzvot expressed their determination to become holy individuals, through the practice of circumcision and holy family units, through membership in the groups that share the Paschal lamb.

They did not stop there. God took them the rest of the distance. He sanctified them, meaning He bestowed the achievement of holiness upon them, something they could never have done on their own. The killing of the firstborn was only a beginning. It led, by the grace of God, to the Chosen People becoming a holy people.

We have wandered a bit. We have more to learn about our own contribution to the journey.

How do we succeed in offering up our own firstborn? Firstly, we take a hint from the death of the Egyptian firstborn, the ridding ourselves of the absolutely negative.

The plague struck at precisely midnight. The *Torat Avot* reminds us that the night has two themes. The first half of the night is the province of the attribute of judgment. The latter half is given to the attribute of compassion.

---

6. Ch. 26.

The two attributes meet at midnight. A Jew will succeed in his quest only if he utilizes both attributes. From our vantage point, judgment evokes fear and reverence in us. Divine compassion inspires us to love God. No one can succeed without using both of these tools in his service of God.

We must take a hard look at the passions of our lives. We can recognize differences among the things that compete for our affections and energies. We regard some of them as intrinsically defensible and important. We understand that some have no redeeming grace, rank, or station. If we are honest, we will recognize that still others are less than human, completely animal-like. We offer no excuses and see them as embarrassing and nonetheless find ourselves unable to extricate ourselves from the clutches of the evil inclination.

We are instructed to find a common fate for all of them. All must be subjugated to God. All must be either discarded or elevated.

There are two ways to do this. One is to subjugate the physical, to break its power through fasting and the like.

There is an alternative. When God enables a person to see more of the light of His Divinity, all other joys and interests pale in comparison. The person understands the worthlessness of his worldly pursuits relative to the sublime beauty of feeling close to Him.

The night before the Exodus incorporated both approaches. The killing of the firstborn weakened the hold of evil. The revelation of the *Shekhina* produced the second effect. It shone a great light, which nullified the appeal of all else.

As we imagine ourselves, the Jews at the time also found themselves wanting in spiritual depth. Our Sages tell us that the attribute of judgment challenged the plan to redeem them. "How do these – the Jews – differ from those – the Egyptians? These worship idols, just as those do!"

God found the solution. He created two mitzvot for them, the blood of the Passover offering and the blood of circumcision. Even when he becomes mired in *tuma*, a Jew continues to struggle. He continues to fight, to spill his blood. He is filled with bitterness over his failures, and continues to battle over two great themes in his inner life, symbolized by those two mitzvot. The blood that the Jews smeared on the doorpost represented their commitment to God, their unshaken belief in Him. (Rashi observes that the blood was placed within the house, visible to the inhabitants, not to the outsiders. A Jew spills his blood in the privacy of the depths of his soul, not before the rest of the world.) The blood of circumcision represented the pursuit of holiness.[7]

These two elements – *emuna* and holiness – are the two foundations of the Jewish home. Some people serve God within the limitations of their personalities, not contravening their natures. This is a mistake. The Exodus required blood. A Jew must learn to spill his blood in his service of God, presenting to Him accomplishments of the greatest difficulty. This is the prescription for all time.

---

7. In other words, all the values of sexual restraint, in conduct and in thought.

The Seventh Day:
Gifts from the Sea

Yisrael saw the great hand that God used upon Egypt. The people feared Hashem, and they believed in Hashem and in Moshe His servant."[1]

What need is there to talk about belief in God after the Torah tells us that the people saw the hand of God? Belief usually fills in when we are unable to know with complete confidence, because the object of our belief remains hidden or inherently unknowable. After God made His existence open and manifest to them through the miracles at the Sea of Reeds, speaking of belief seems tautological.

There is another reason why the Torah should not speak here of the people's *emuna*. They were hardly new to steadfast belief in God. Well before the crossing of the Sea of Reeds they had believed. It was, in fact "in the merit of belief that our forefathers were redeemed from Egypt."[2] Having already believed at an earlier time, why does the Torah take note of it here?

Based on *Netivot Shalom* 2:281–283.

1. Ex. 14:31.
2. *Yalkut Shimoni, Hoshea*, 519.

Belief, we must begin to realize, is not a simple response to a yes-or-no question. It is complex, variegated, nuanced. It knows many levels, each of which is an important accomplishment.

Two of these are fairly apparent to us. We can easily understand the difference between believing something with one's mind and believing it in one's heart. (The *Yesod HaAvoda* cites a disciple of the Maggid of Mezeritch who claimed that the distance between belief of the mind and the belief of the heart is greater than the distance between heaven and earth.)

We should add to these a third kind of *emuna* – believing with one's body. "All my limbs will proclaim, God – who is like You?"[3] When *emuna* matures, it penetrates all parts of a person's body. Every fiber of him understands that there is nothing besides God.

Picture in your mind's eye a person you know has great belief in God. Now imagine him overcome by an unexpected terror, thrust instantly into a life-threatening situation. Does he not act troubled? Does he not tremble and shake? He would not if belief thoroughly suffused all his body. He would remain calm and unperturbed.[4]

In his first dialogue with God, Moshe challenged God. "What if the Jews will not believe me?"[5] God reassured him that they would show themselves to be believers. *Emuna* is firmly rooted in the Jewish soul, a dependable legacy from our ancestors. Its presence within us can be relied upon with confidence. (Rabbi Noah of Leuḥovitz had

---

3. Ps. 35:10.
4. Rabbi Yaakov Kamenetsky once recalled the time that czarist agents scoured his village for military recruits. His parents hid him under the floorboards of their house. As he heard them approach, he began shaking – and could not stop for hours after they left. Building on that experience, he asked about the angel who stopped Avraham's hand at the *Akeda*, the Binding of Yitzḥak. The angel said, "Now I know that you are a God-fearing man." Why just then? Had he not seen the terror on Avraham's face before? There are two kinds of fear, explained Rabbi Yaakov. One is destructive and debilitating and plainly visible to all. A higher form, though, is satisfying and inspiring. We must visualize Avraham wearing a smile on the way to the *Akeda*. His fear of God did not make him tremble or leave his brow furrowed. His outward appearance, therefore, did not evidence fear of God, and the angel had to wait until his hand was poised to fulfill God's instruction.
5. Exodus 4:1.

this advice for a Jew who claimed that he could not feel *emuna* working within him. "You should believe that you believe! Clouds cover the light of your *emuna* and darken your world.")

This belief, this birthright from our ancestors, while powerful and cherished, is still incomplete. A nation of believers left Egypt. Their belief was of the usual varieties, belief of the mind and the heart. Because it was not of the absolutely highest order of *emuna*, the Egyptians were still able to pursue them with their chariots and hordes. Pharaoh himself was able to "draw close"[6] – his impending attack disoriented and confounded them. They reacted with fear and cried out to God.

All this changed at the Sea of Reeds. When the Jews saw their persecutors lying dead before them, when they saw the great hand outstretched mightily against their enemy, they grew immeasurably in their belief. "There remained of them [the Egyptians] not a single one."[7] This does not just mean that all the soldiers died, but alludes to the complete devastation of Egypt in a spiritual sense. It means that the *kelipa*, the spiritual miasma enveloping Egypt, had been shattered and smashed. When this happened, Benei Yisrael were able to traverse the distance to the far end of the *emuna*-continuum.

How did they achieve this elevation? Belief in mind and heart were all that was necessary for them to escape the Egyptian borders. Standing at the edge of the sea, the ground rumbling as the fastest chariots approached, they cried out to God. Moshe took their cry to God, and He offered only one route. They were told to move on, to jump into the water.

The miracles at the Sea of Reeds began only when their bodies and minds acted in concert. *Emuna* needed to enter their physical being, not just their psychic space. They rose to the level of belief with their bodies.

We can explain the difference in their belief – before and after the Splitting of the Sea – in yet other terms. The Baal Shem Tov once said, "After all the levels I have achieved, after all the things I have comprehended, I am but a simple youngster in belief." We are mystified by this

---

6. Ibid. 14:10.
7. Ibid. 14:28.

declaration. What room is left for "belief" after reaching the clarity of the Baal Shem Tov? He understood – he surely did not need to believe!

This is an error. The mitzva of *emuna* relates to everyone. It applied to the Baal Shem Tov and it applied to Moshe, who encountered, as it were, the true countenance of God, and understood more than other human beings.

God is called *Ein Sof* – without end. Whenever we think that we have grasped some new insight into what He is, we realize how much more there is that we do not understand. This process is endless.

Emuna transcends all levels of comprehension. We need it not so much for the insights and intuitions about God that we possess to some degree, but for the vastness of what we do not understand. Moshe, the Baal Shem Tov, grasped much. But much of what God is eluded them. They – and we – need *emuna* to relate to what we sense is remote and incomprehensible.

While still in Egypt, the Jews believed. They believed within the context of an arena they had entered earlier and with which they were familiar. At the Sea of Reeds, their understanding soared. But at the same time, they were able to *believe* in levels they knew nothing of at all.

Having come this far, there is still something elusive and troublesome in the order of the verses describing Jewish reaction to the Splitting of the Sea. "Yisrael saw Egypt dead on the seashore. Israel saw the great hand that God used against Egypt."[8] This seems to be an inversion. The great hand brought the sea crashing down at the right moment. They saw it churn up from the deep those Egyptians who were the most guilty, so that they could be punished longer. It was only later that the bodies of the Egyptians were cast up on the shore. Why are these two images presented out of chronological order?

Above, we posited that the essential Exodus was the escape from the Egyptian *kelipa*. So far, we have considered only one of its effects. Pharaoh's initial exchange with Moshe showed him mocking the existence of God. Pharaoh was a non-believer; his disbelief was part of the *kelipa*. Jewish belief was its antidote, and for this reason, the Sages pointed to it as the cause of their redemption.

---

8. Ex. 14:30–31.

The Egyptian poison had another form as well. Egypt was also the "nakedness of the land."[9] It was a place of complete moral depravity, the polar opposite of Jewish holiness.

Belief and holiness are a matched set. They are not only the foundational elements of Jewish life, but they are interdependent. A person's belief will be clouded and marred if he does not purify his conduct and experience personal holiness. On the other hand, it is difficult to motivate oneself to live a holier life without the impetus of clear *emuna*.

The Exodus was only the beginning of Jewish redemption. Through their *emuna*, the Jews left, having escaped the *kelipa* of rejection and disbelief. The remaining Egyptian weapon of mass spiritual destruction – the negation of holiness – remained intact.

"What did the sea observe that it split? It saw the casket of Yosef."[10] Yosef's escape from the clutches of Potiphar's wife is the symbol of the triumph of holiness over the spiritually tawdry and ugly, of personal morality over personal corruption. What the Exodus was to *emuna* the Splitting of the Sea was to holiness. Here, the second element of the *kelipa* was humbled and destroyed. As holiness triumphed, Jewish *emuna* was able to surge forward. The process of redemption, begun a week before, could now proceed.

The verses we considered are really not reversed. To be sure, the great hand of God operated well before the Egyptians lay dead. What changed was how much of that hand the Jews appreciated. Since *emuna*, belief, and *kedusha*, holiness, are linked, the completeness of their belief had to await the death of the Egyptians, which we understand to mean the shattering of the *kelipa* of unholiness and impurity. From that point on, blinders on their belief were removed. They now not only sensed His great hand with their intellects, but they understood it as clearly as something manifest, obvious, and visible. Looking back, they *saw* His great hand.

Each holiday offers us easier access to something that is ordinarily harder to attain. Passover is the holiday of *emuna*. Its first day is

9. Gen. 42:9.
10. *Yalkut Shimoni, Tehillim* 873.

a Rosh HaShana of belief. The seventh day is the holiday of advanced, perfected belief.

Our Sages tell us that the Jews of the Exodus enriched themselves by despoiling the Egyptian army that was cast up from the sea. Surrounded by his Hasidim on the last day of Passover, the Saba Kadisha of Slonim asked them if they, too, would like to share in that wealth. An old Hasid replied affirmatively. "We want the belief that the Jews gained at the sea." The rebbe praised the response. There is no greater gift than clarity of belief at the highest level. Nothing can make man happier. It is the true richness that we took away from the sea.

We emphasize on the Seder night that "in every generation, a person is obligated to see himself as if he exited Egypt." On the seventh night of Passover, each person should see himself crossing through the Sea of Reeds. He should take advantage of the treasures this day offers.

The *Beit Avraham* argues that the seventh day of Passover holds promise for all the aspects of life that can be described as "as difficult as the Splitting of the Sea."[11] Certainly, the fullness of belief and holiness are among those aspects.

Each year, the seventh day of Passover allows a Jew the opportunity to burst all the barriers that divide him from his Creator. With their disappearance, we come closer to where we belong and where all difficulties vanish.

---

11. Pesaḥim 118a.

Sefirat HaOmer

The Diminutive Omer

Through the mitzva of the Omer offering, Avraham merited the land."[1] So says the midrash. This is confusing. Our recollection is that the Omer is nowhere to be found in the Torah's narrative about God's promise to Avraham.

The midrash is even more confusing in its full form. It warns us not to view the Omer "lightly," because it was through it that Avraham inherited the land. To prove the point, the midrash cites two verses that appear serially. The first[2] promises the land to Avraham and his descendants; the next exhorts him to "keep My covenant." The midrash sees the first verse as predicated upon the second – you will merit the land only because you continue to keep the covenant. The entire section and the covenant referenced therein, however, clearly refer to the mitzva of circumcision. Circumcision is the covenant upon which the promise of the land is contingent. How this midrash sees an allusion to the Omer is mystifying.

Based on *Netivot Shalom* 2:322–324.
1. Leviticus Rabba 28:6.
2. Gen. 17:8.

We will put our main question aside for the moment and return to it later. First, let us consider the truism that very few people maintain an even keel in relating to Torah and mitzvot. We are blessed at times with periods of great clarity and enlightenment. They are usually not permanent but give way to times of limited grasp. Worse yet, we sometimes find that our minds are so beclouded that our visibility is reduced to near zero. These periods of greatness and smallness are called in Kabbala *gadlut hamoḥin* and *katnut hamoḥin.*[3]

We are commanded to perform the mitzva of circumcision on an eight-day-old child. The infant has no higher-order comprehension at that early stage in his life. Neither his mind nor his body has yet matured. He could be a poster boy for *katnut hamoḥin*. Yet it is this mitzva in particular that safeguards our right to the land – which in turn is the gateway to the highest levels of comprehension.

What circumcision is to the individual, the Omer is to the nation. It recalls the collective level of our people upon emerging from Egypt, stepping into physical freedom from the forty-ninth rung on the scale of degradation. It is for this reason that the Omer is brought from barley, which served as animal fodder in ancient times. At the time we offer it, we are still animal-like and not quite human. The Omer represents the most reduced form of national attainment, and yet it serves as the necessary precursor to the encounter with God seven weeks later at Sinai. Each year's journey of forty-nine days begins with a single offering that bespeaks inadequacy but brings the nation to the doorstep of prophecy.

So perhaps the connection between circumcision and the Omer is not so mystifying. Circumcision and the Omer share an apparent minimalism: they both seem to be mitzvot performed with a deficit of spiritual input. The midrash's lesson is uplifting and powerful. From these two examples we learn not to cynically dismiss the mitzvot we perform during the times of our lives that lack clarity and focus. These mitzvot make minimal demands and place limited expectation upon those who observe them. Yet each of them leads to extraordinarily great things: to

---

3. Literally, greatness of the intellects and smallness of the intellects. The primary meaning of "intellects" is the highest three *sefirot* in the system of ten.

earning the Land of Israel and to receiving the Torah. How foolish it would be to doubt the power of any mitzva, even one performed in a state of spiritual weakness.

The Omer shows its small footprint in the arena of blessings as well. Unlike with so many other mitzvot, we do not recite the *Sheheḥeyanu* blessing on the counting of the Omer. One explanation utilizes the famous observation of the Ari regarding the relationship between the first night of Passover and the Omer period: All the spiritual lights and revelations that we try to grab hold of in the run-up to Shavuot are actually present on the Seder night, only to be withdrawn after the first day of Passover. While they return, one at a time, in the following weeks, none of them are really new. The *Sheheḥeyanu* blessing is restricted to new items; the period of *Sefirat HaOmer*, the counting of the Omer, deals exclusively, as it were, in old merchandise.

This approach yields a new interpretation of the wise son's question: the *avoda* that he questions is that which happens during the period of *Sefirat HaOmer*. "Look here," he remarks, "why are you commanded to participate in an elaborate *avoda* during *sefira*? It doesn't get you anything new. Everything that you work toward, you already had in hand on the first night of Passover!"

We explain to him that we must always be ready to put something away for *afikoman*, referring to the matza that is eaten at the end of the Passover Seder. A vast richness of spiritual light bursts out on the night of the Seder, a display of the *itaruta dele'eila* of the holiday. Through the mitzvot of the evening, we carry over those lights to the following day, the first day of Passover. Beyond that, however, lies a period of time of relative concealment. The wealth of light is lost; it is made available to us sequentially, one light at a time.

We spend much of our lives following the same pattern. We are privileged to experience some times of great enlightenment, but we experience the opposite as well. We survive the darkness by planning for it in advance – by salting away some of the light for the spiritual night-time, just as we set aside the *afikoman* for the end of the Seder. This is the intent of the calendric link between Passover and Tisha B'Av, in which the latter always falls on the same day of the week as the Seder night. The Torah's message is that we can capture enough of the spiritual gift of the first night of Passover to remain bound to God at the times of the densest fog and gloom, like Tisha B'Av.

This, then, is the special promise of the *Sefirat HaOmer* period. We discover the richness of leftovers, of how much remains accessible to us from those momentary bursts of brilliance. We see how to take them, build with them, until we become different, elevated people, ready to stand once again at the base of the mountain of Revelation.

Completing the Incomplete

Passover and Shavuot are strangely adrift in the calendar. Take dates, for instance. For some reason, the Torah fails to attach a calendar date to the mitzva of bringing the Omer offering. Similarly, it doesn't link Shavuot to a specific date. (The Omer is mysteriously described as obligatory on "the day after Shabbat;"[1] Shavuot is simply called the fiftieth day.[2]) Why do the starting and finishing points of the Omer period lack their own identities?

In truth, the season is all about completing the incomplete, about a process that gets started around Passover but remains unfinished until it matures on Shavuot.

This process takes place in different ways and on different levels, but the underlying theme is the same: Passover, Shavuot, and the period in between amount to a single conceptual event, stretched over time.

Based on *Netivot Shalom* 2:311–313.

1. Lev. 23:15.
2. Ibid. 23:16.

Freedom itself grows and matures during this period. It is true that Passover gives us plenty to celebrate. Freedom is no small gift; on Passover we were freed from the dominion of the Egyptians and from the oppressiveness of their spiritual suffocation of our forebears. The progression from Passover to Shavuot, however, emphasizes that we did not fully earn our freedom when we triumphantly crossed out of Egypt. Full freedom comes only with Shavuot and acceptance of the Torah; no person is free without Torah. On the other hand, no one can arrive at a proper acceptance of the Torah without the weeks-long inner purification that ought to be taking place between the two holidays. (These observations can explain why the mitzva of happiness is not mentioned in connection with Passover, even though the Torah does explicitly mention this mitzva in regard to the other two pilgrimage festivals.[3] Our Sages are left to derive the happiness obligation on Passover exegetically from its mention in association with Shavuot and Sukkot. By this the Torah hints to us that the full measure of Passover's happiness cannot be experienced on Passover. Only the person who uses the time between Passover and Shavuot to slowly and methodically mend his character can achieve true joy.)

Our growth in the period of the counting of the Omer takes place in two distinct ways. The first is in distancing ourselves from the clutches of Egypt. Earlier works point out that the Exodus is mentioned exactly fifty times in the Torah. We do not achieve true freedom in a single moment. Leaving Egypt was the first step; many, many more steps needed to follow. (The reference to the Benei Yisrael going up from Egypt "*hamushim*"[4] can be taken this way. When they left Egypt, they went merely one-fiftieth of the distance toward freedom that they needed to go.)

The Torah describes the count of the Omer as "fifty days,"[5] even though we stop the count at forty-nine. The explanation, according to our approach, is straightforward. The count begins with and includes the

---

3. Deut. 16:11, 14.
4. Ex. 13:18. The word is related to the number five.
5. Lev. 23:16.

first step, on the first day of Passover. While we do not include it formally in our count, it is the all-important first step that launches the journey.

Understood more precisely and kabbalistically, on the first day of Passover, the various "lights" of redemption that are revealed by God's closeness are all flashed in an instant, shining from the uppermost *sefirot*. It seems to us that these divine lights are being offered to us willy-nilly. After the first day, those *sefirot* become hidden from us. We are left to pick up the pieces, as it were, finding the vestiges of those lights and assembling them in the proper order, one at a time, one day at a time. The burden is upon us to search them out and incorporate them within ourselves. When we complete the process, we are ready for a Shavuot just as potent in divine revelation as the Passover that preceded it.

The second crucial dimension of our growth addresses our character. Purifying our character traits provides the vehicle for receiving the Torah, because all our inner imperfections prevent Torah from taking up a firm position within us. The *gematria* of forty-nine, the number of days between Passover and Shavuot, equals that of *lev tov*, a good heart. (While the five students of R. Yoḥanan b. Zakkai each suggested a different focus of self-development, it was R. Elazar b. Arakh's contribution of *lev tov* that won out in the mishna.)[6] The heart, after all, is the seat of all the character traits. The Maharal teaches that man must perfect himself in three crucial kinds of interaction: with God, with other people, and with himself. While improving character traits is always important, the work is especially pressing during this period, when we ready ourselves for our impending acceptance of the Torah.

The *Beit Avraham* noted the serendipity in the Torah readings during the weeks of *Sefirat HaOmer*. They begin with an inventory of human failings: *nega'im*, or physical blemishes stemming from spiritual malady, *tuma*, and *arayot*, or improper relationships. They then move to the holiness that can take root, once those faults have been eliminated. The Torah speaks of the general mitzva of pursuing holiness (*Kedoshim tihyu*)[7]. It delineates specific instructions for sanctifying our eating, our intimacy, our communal representatives (the priests), time

---

6. Mishna Avot 2:13.
7. Lev. 19:2.

(the holidays), and our land. We come to realize that holiness is not a laudatory refinement that we add on to proper living, but part of the very essence of being Jewish.

Some are puzzled by the manner in which the Torah instructs us in the mitzva of the two loaves offering on Shavuot. "You shall count fifty days and offer a new *minḥa* to Hashem."[8] The Torah first mentions the offering obliquely, simply calling it a "new *minḥa*" but offering no details. It then provides a full description of the offering in the following verses. Why the generalized introduction of "new *minḥa*"? And why link that generic description to the counting of the Omer rather than to the holiday of Shavuot?

The puzzle is solved. The very point of the counting is to make the two kinds of change that we have been talking about. When we complete this process, we ourselves become the new *minḥa*. The *Keli Yakar* explains that the offering on Shavuot is called "new" because it is emblematic of Torah, which our Sages tell us must be new in our eyes each day. We spend seven weeks between Passover and Shavuot completing and ordering the lights of revelation that briefly flashed within us on the first night of Passover and finishing the housecleaning of our inner selves and character. This allows us to take part each year in a new acceptance of the Torah, an experience that will be only as rich and fulfilling as the effort that went into improving our conduct in this special period of time.

---

8. Ibid. 23:16.

Pesaḥ Sheni: Gates Closing and Opening

The Zohar[1] takes an underappreciated day and turns it into a conundrum. Liberally paraphrased, the Zohar says that *Knesset Yisrael*, having been adorned with crowns in the month of Nisan, retains its regal trappings for a full thirty days after the beginning of Passover. As long as *Knesset Yisrael* remains so outfitted, the *sefira* of *malkhut*[2] remains potentiated and accessible. With the end of these thirty days, a heavenly message announces that those who were unable to take advantage of this opportunity to engage the *sefira* of *malkhut* earlier are now warned that they have seven more days to take a deeper look at this heavenly treasure. After that, the gates close. This warning is issued on *Pesaḥ Sheni*.

Questions abound. What special quality does this period of accessibility have? Is it supposed to last for thirty days – the period of

---

Based on *Netivot Shalom* 2:324–326.

1. Zohar 3:152b.
2. The Zohar's text reads: "beholding the *Matronita*." The term often means some level of the *sefira* of *malkhut*.

the wearing of the "crowns" – or thirty-seven? If it is thirty, which is the impression one gets from reading the source, what are the seven bonus days about? Is it not ironic that the gates close two weeks before Shavuot, as we would expect the gates to open wider yet before our annual reliving of the receiving of the Torah?

Questions abound regarding the source of *Pesaḥ Sheni* as well. The people who agitated for another chance at offering a Paschal lamb are described by the Torah as "unable"[3] to bring their offering at the proper time. This is not quite accurate. They were not so much unable as not allowed. Additionally, what was their argument in stating, "Why should we be lessened by not offering God's offering at its appointed time among the Children of Israel?"[4] They knew quite well why they were in a deficient position. They were spiritually impure; they had articulated as much themselves. They understood the law that their impure state barred their participation in the mitzva of the Paschal lamb. Why would they see themselves as unfairly excluded when they knew that they were like any other person who, through no fault of his own, lacked some of the prerequisite conditions for performing a mitzva properly?

The Torah instructs us regarding the retelling of the Passover story on the Seder night, "And you will relate it to your son *on that day.*" The Ari saw a parallel between the last phrase of that sentence and the vision with which we conclude the *Aleinu* prayer, "And it will be that Hashem will be King over all the earth. *On that day,* God will be One and His name will be One."[5] Awesome revelations of God and His ways will accompany our day of redemption and deliverance when the Messiah arrives. The parallel phraseology informs us that those revelations are all available to us on some level each year on the Seder night as well.

Those in the wilderness who were impure had good reason to complain, at least on an emotional level. They understood the potential of the Seder night and its revelations; they could not accept that they would be denied the boost to their spirituality that everyone else experienced. (In fact, they were disadvantaged relative to people in comparable

---

3. Num. 9:6.
4. Ibid. 9:7.
5. Zech. 14:9.

positions. The complainants were all, according to the tradition of our Sages,[6] on their very last day of the process of purification after being defiled by a corpse, with all requirements fulfilled other than waiting out the clock until evening. In all other situations, the priest can slaughter an offering on behalf of someone whose purification requirements are satisfied and that person need only wait for evening before returning to the status of purity. The Paschal lamb, however, differs from other offerings in that it ushers in the exalted spiritual revelations of the Seder night. Any vestige whatsoever of defilement from a corpse is incompatible with this revelatory experience; hence the exceptional exclusion.)

To be sure, the revelations of the Seder night revolve around the special character of the time – the moment at which the Jewish people were chosen as special and therefore singled out for the loving relationship God demonstrated at the time of the Exodus. Each year, a Jewish soul begins the journey toward this moment of elevation a full thirty days before Passover. On each of those thirty days, the soul leaves behind another level of degradation, until it has unburdened itself of much negativity by the fifteenth of Nisan. But rejecting the unseemly in the soul is very different from achieving positive growth. Only the elevation of the soul through holiness makes a person worthy of the distinction of being part of a chosen people. This elevation occurs through making good use of the revealed lights of the Seder night. During the thirty days that follow, we continue to draw from them, consolidating our hold on them within us. This is what the Zohar means by beholding the *Matrunisa*.[7]

The availability of these lights ends after thirty days. The experience is so crucial, however, that God in His compassion does not wish to see anyone left out. Precisely when the gates close on the lights of Passover, a message goes out that He has opened a new gate specifically designed for those who were locked out of the first. (No herald had to announce the first thirty days. Those who were positioned properly felt the revelation of the night of Passover and simply had to hold onto and draw from their presence for the next month. By contrast, on *Pesah Sheni*, a second chance is announced for those who until then had been

---

6. Pesaḥim 90b.
7. See above, note 3.

moved to the sidelines.) This is a truism about God's providence. As we say during *Ne'ila* on Yom Kippur, "Open for us a gate at the time of the closing of the gate." Whenever God closes off one avenue of approach, He opens a new one, even if briefly, to allow for last-minute joiners.

Today, we regrettably have neither the Paschal lamb nor its substitute on *Pesaḥ Sheni*. It would be mistaken, however, to see *Pesaḥ Sheni* as a theoretical construct of mostly historical interest. All parts of Torah continue to function on some level in all time periods; the special days come with the same regularity, along with their special gifts.

Two categories of people are unable to participate in the Paschal lamb and are shunted to *Pesaḥ sheni*: those who are impure and those who are distant from Jerusalem. These categories represent two kinds of spiritual deficit within us today. Some people have defiled themselves; they have become impure. They come up short in areas of holiness. Others find themselves distanced from the power of Jerusalem. Their problem lies in deficient *emuna*.

Holiness and *emuna*, of course, are the two pillars of Jewish living. God provides a second chance for those who might otherwise miss out. *Pesaḥ Sheni* beckons to all of us to accept the divine hand that is extended, just as we think it is drawing away.

Shavuot

You Can't Do It Alone

He is our Father. Yet not a single one of us is His child. Impossible? Not really. In the solution to this puzzle lies a key element in our preparation for Shavuot.

It is patently clear that no person is called God's child. Only collectively are we ever referred to as His children, as in *"Banim atem Lashem,"* "You (plural) are children to Hashem." Similarly, He is never called Father to the individual but only to the collective – and only when united as one. Think of the words at the end of the *Amida*. "Bless us, our Father, all of us as one." The last words emphasize that God assumes the special role of Father only in regard to us as a whole, and additionally, only when we are united.

We do not have to look very hard to find other examples of specialness attached to the collective. The mitzva of Shabbat was given to us with all of us gathered together to receive it,[1] unlike most other mitzvot. The instruction to strive for holiness was also given in the Torah as a command to the many, not to the individual: "You are to sanctify

---

Based on *Netivot Shalom* 2:355–357.

1. Ex. 35:1.

yourselves, and you shall be holy."[2] What do these two mitzvot, Shabbat and the commandment to be holy, share in common? They both involve unusual levels of attachment to the Divine. Individuals simply can't achieve this kind of attachment on their own. Only the many, the community, can access these lofty gifts. More precisely, they both deal with attainment that exceeds the "natural." The individual does not have it within his power to transcend the natural. The special power of the collective makes such transcendence possible.

As we approach Shavuot, Benei Yisrael's acceptance of the Torah springs to mind as an example of this principle. "And Israel encamped there, opposite the mountain."[3] The *Mekhilta* famously tells us that the verse employs the singular form of the verb for "encamped" to indicate that they encamped "with one heart, as one being." We take this even further in the Shabbat *zemirot*: "All of the entered, together, into a covenant; they all said, '*Naase venishma*,' 'We will do and we will listen,' as one." Banding together gave them the ability to make the most perfect declaration in human history – *naase venishma*.

The mind-set behind that declaration is *hitbatlut* – negating the sense of self in the presence of God.[4] This, of course, is easier said than done. In imagining how we could get there, we quickly see the place of the collective. Becoming part of a collective requires that we diminish our sense of self, our assumption that we are beings of real inherent value. This imagined substance of ours is toxic to our relationship with others. So long as this sense of substance survives within us, it dictates how we interact with everyone else. It demands to be fed and pampered, making it difficult to truly join in with others to serve the common good.

Benei Yisrael found unity in encamping at the foot of Mount Sinai. People threw themselves into the collective for that event, subduing their sense of self-importance by negating it relative to the nation. Through this *hitbatlut* to something outside of their individual selves, they were then able to negate themselves before God and declare *naase venishma*.

---

2. Lev. 11:44.
3. Ex. 19:2.
4. See the next chapter, "Relating the Power of the Evening."

The Gemara[5] describes a heavenly voice exclaiming at the time, "Who revealed to My children this secret, which the ministering angels use?" The angels' "secret" is their complete *hitbatlut* to the will of God. This is not difficult for them; they lack a sense of self that would interfere with it. Humans, on the other hand, have a developed sense of self. Negating it, achieving what the angels do with ease, is a remarkable accomplishment.

We find no other preparation by our ancestors for the giving of the Torah – only the all-important negation of self that began with their joining together at the foot of the mountain. Keeping this in mind, we arrive at a new understanding of a practice that the kabbalistic works urge upon us. They tell us before every prayer to consciously accept upon ourselves to love our fellow as ourselves. The reason may be not that the mitzva of loving others is so important, but that it is impossible to really love the next person without first conquering our sense of self. At the core of the mitzva of loving the other, then, is *hitbatlut*. This *hitbatlut*, achieved in some measure by our focusing upon it momentarily in our preparation for prayer, maximizes its effectiveness and power.

Rabbi Akiva called loving our fellow as ourselves "the great principle of the Torah."[6] Why is this true? In what sense does this mitzva stand out from among all the important mitzvot of the Torah? Furthermore, it is not at all clear that loving our neighbor should be seen as important on the continuum of mitzvot. It might be more accurate to view it as off the charts! This is because it has a special role as a prerequisite for the performance of mitzvot.

Rabbi Ḥayim Vital makes this very clear. He explains why the Torah does not explicitly direct us in the work of character refinement. He says that it is not that this work is unimportant. To the contrary, it is so important that it must come before mitzva observance. The Torah simply cannot impress its most positive imprint upon a person with unrefined character. Addressing our character flaws is thus a precondition to employing the system of mitzvot, not a part of it. Loving our fellow would seem to us to be part of the labor of improving the inner person, and therefore not at all a "great principle" of the body of the Torah.

---

5. Shabbat 88a.
6. Y. Nedarim 9:4.

Rabbi Akiva may have something quite different in mind. The "great principle" is not in the mitzva of loving others itself, but in the *hitbatlut*, the self-effacement that must precede loving others properly. This *hitbatlut* is indeed the great principle that allows a person to perform his individual acceptance of the Torah. We remove the ego-barriers in our relationship with God most effectively by first learning to do the same with regard to other human beings.

Each year, as we approach Shavuot and ready ourselves for receiving the Torah anew, we should keep in mind the need to band together with all other Jews, becoming as one with the many.

Relating the Power
of the Evening

One of the most emotionally wrenching parts of the prayers of the Days of Awe is *Unetaneh Tokef*, which bids us to "relate the power of the holiness of the day." Paraphrasing just a bit, we should likewise talk about the power of a remarkable evening, the evening of Shavuot.

In some ways, the night of Shavuot is the most elevated and exalted of all nights of the year. The *Peri Etz Ḥayim* of the Ari tells us that a person's entire direction in life is tied to this evening. The kabbalistic works illuminate this statement by explaining the connection between the night of Shavuot and the process of perfecting the *sefirot*, which is a theme of the weeks between Passover and Shavuot. In the space of forty-nine days, we address each *sefira* and its interconnection with all the others. Standing, so to speak, above all of them is the highest of all elements in this system, *keter*. Its turn for *tikkun*, rectification, comes on

---

Based on *Netivot Shalom* 2:342–343.

the night of Shavuot. (The process is fully completed with the recitation of *Keter*[1] in the *Kedusha* prayer of *Musaf* the next day.)

On a more down-to-earth level, what we need to do on this night is straightforward. We call Shavuot "the time of the giving of our Torah." We mean this in the here and now, not in the past. As all things in the Torah are eternal, the giving of the Torah is a permanent fixture on the calendar. We receive the Torah anew each year on the sixth of Sivan. The evening of Shavuot is our preparation for the giving of the Torah that will take place the following day.

The Exodus took place, Kabbala teaches us, through an *itaruta dele'eila.* All of its important elements were accomplished by God. Even the spiritual elevation we needed as a prerequisite for leaving was engineered through His reaching out to us.

God reminds us of this in the run-up to the Revelation. He briefly recounts the events of the Exodus and stresses His singular role in it. "You have seen what *I* did to Egypt, and that *I* have borne you on the wings of eagles and *I* brought you to Me."[2] The emphasis changes as He shifts focus to the giving of the Torah. "And now if *you* will listen to My voice…"[3] Receiving the Torah required an *itaruta deletata,* an spiritual awakening of themselves from within.

What could this awakening have been? What did they need to do to prepare themselves? Was there some particular merit they needed to acquire? Our Sages tell us that our forefathers were redeemed from Egypt in the merit of their faith. What merit did the giving of the Torah require?

The Haggada states that there would have been sufficient grounds to thank God had He brought us to Sinai, even had He not followed that with giving us the Torah. We are told, by way of explanation, that Adam's first sin introduced an essential corruption of the human spirit and our gathering at Sinai undid that.[4] This deepens our question. What did man do that enabled him to rid himself of this

---

1. According to *nusaḥ Sepharad.*
2. Ex. 19:4.
3. Ibid. 19:5.
4. It was, unfortunately, reintroduced through the sin of the Golden Calf.

ancient burden? If we find the answer, we might know what we in turn are expected to accomplish on this all-important night of anticipating the giving of the Torah.

When the Jews pledged, "We will do," before agreeing, "We will listen," six hundred thousand ministering angels, according to the Gemara,[5] descended and placed two crowns on each Jew's head, one for each of the two phrases. Our Sages also report that a heavenly voice called out, "Who revealed this great secret to My children, a secret ordinarily used by the angels themselves!"

In the unparalleled drama of this episode, we can detect the answer to our question. The preceding of "we will listen" with "we will do" was itself the necessary preparation and prerequisite for the Revelation of the Torah.

That worked once in history but doesn't leave much room for an encore. Yet, if we distill this response conceptually, we realize that it can be repeated, in some form or other, every year. For Benei Yisrael to say this with conviction required *hitbatlut*, complete self-negation before the presence of God.[6] Each Jew who answered in this way promised to perform the will of God without any preconditions. No one predicated his acceptance upon finding Torah reasonable or emotionally and spiritually fulfilling. They would all perform, simply because God asked them to.

This is no small achievement, but the highest form of serving Him. (We are familiar with it from other sources. The *Kedushat Levi* argues that an all-important part of repentance is that the sinner feel a sense of negation of self before God.) At Sinai, Jews were able to feel a sense of relative nothingness in the presence of God. Only by becoming nothing could they attach themselves fully to God. That which is fully attached to the *Tahor* itself becomes *tahor*. This is the fuller explanation of how they shed the primordial corruption of man.

Negation is the key to understanding other statements of our Sages. They tell us, for example, that the Torah was given with "dread, awe,

---

5. Shabbat 88a.
6. See the previous chapter, "You Can't Do It Alone."

trembling, and fear."[7] As long as a Jew lives in the darkness of physical existence, he fails to see the greatness of the Creator. Walking in blindness, he will feel nothing – no dread, no awe, no trembling, and no fear. By placing "We will do" up front before "We will listen," the Jews negated their interests, negated themselves, and loosened the restrictive bonds that physical existence ordinarily imposes. For the first time they could see clearly – as clearly as one sees with his eyes – the greatness of God. Then they could not help but feel awe and reverence.

Elsewhere, our Sages describe the utter silence at Sinai. "No bird chirped; no wing took flight; no ox lowed. The *ofanim* did not soar; the *serafim*[8] ceased their calling 'Kadosh.' The sea was entirely calm; people did not speak. The world waited in complete silence as the voice of God carried forth, 'I am Hashem your God …'"[9] Not only the Jews assembled at the base of the mountain listened in absolute awe, but all existence became still and motionless. As the Jews succeeded in negating themselves to the Divine, some of their achievement spilled over to their surroundings, and the world at large ceased to possess an identity of its own. Nothing asserted its own existence; existence itself was manifest only in God Himself.

The crucial preparation for receiving the Torah through *hitbatlut* required its own preparation. "And Yisrael encamped there, opposite the mountain."[10] The text uses the singular form for the verb "encamped." Our Sages comment that Benei Yisrael succeeded in functioning as and becoming a single entity, with one heart and purpose, joined together as if in a single person. *Hitbatlut* is not within reach of most individuals; banding together as a community places it within our grasp.

The spiritual backdrop to the final hours before each year's receiving of the Torah is the *tikkun* reaching all the way to the *sefira* of *keter*. In the human sphere, we accomplish this by scaling the highest peak of achievement – leaving us not with an exhilarated feeling about ourselves, but rather giving us the freedom to yield ourselves entirely to Him.

---

7. Berakhot 22a.
8. *Ofanim* and *serafim* are two kinds of angels.
9. Exodus Rabba 29:9.
10. Ex. 19:2.

Two Loaves, Two Methods

Y ou don't need a degree in higher mathematics to do the computation. From the dates given by the Torah for the Exodus and for the receiving of the Torah at Sinai, we quickly confirm that the holiday of Shavuot coincides with the date that Benei Yisrael stood ready to receive the Torah. You couldn't tell, however, from the Torah's description of the holiday. It doesn't say anything about the giving of the Torah. More frustratingly, perhaps, the Torah highlights a different event while bypassing the Revelation.

"And you shall offer a new *minḥa*-offering to God. From your dwelling places you shall bring bread that shall be waved, two loaves of two tenths of an *epha*; they shall be of fine flour, baked as *ḥametz, bikkurim* (first fruits) to Hashem."[1] The giving of the Torah is passed over. The front-and-center position of the Torah's description of Shavuot is occupied by the *shtei haleḥem*, the two-loaves offering.

Equally disturbing is the insistence that the offering come in the form of *ḥametz*. It is as if the Passover we are told to count from has receded so far in our memory that we now embrace what was shunned

---

Based on *Netivot Shalom* 2:359–361.
1. Lev. 23:16–17.

so absolutely during the previous holiday. It was only a matter of weeks since we were instructed to ferret out every last morsel of *hametz*; on Shavuot it makes a dramatic and unexpected comeback. When we remember that we explained away our preoccupation with *hametz* crumbs as symbolic of the evil inclination, whose every last vestige we wished to banish, the turnaround on Shavuot is all the more surprising. Why would we want to invite back in what previously was a banned substance?

We round out our list of difficulties by noting that something about the Torah's description of the offering seems a bit off. Why does the Torah refer to is as a "new *minha*-offering"? There is nothing new about the offering as a *minha*. It obeys rules similar to other *minha* offerings. What makes it new is the use of the new crop of grain. We would expect the Torah to call it a "*minha* of new grain."

Our Sages make a puzzling assertion about the generation of the wilderness: "The Torah was given only to those who ate the manna."[2] Our tradition regarding the manna is that it was a gourmand's delight; you could taste in it whatever you fancied. While this may be attractive to us, it flies in the face of what we are taught about the necessary sacrifices one must be prepared to make in order to acquire Torah. The Mishna in Avot[3] tells us that the way of Torah is to eat plain bread flavored only with salt. A passage in the Gemara[4] argues that Torah gains a firm foothold only with those who kill themselves over it. Why would the Torah be given to those who dined on a table of earthly delights?

We might find a solution in a comment of the *Peri Haaretz*.[5] In describing the rabble that complained about the manna, clamoring for meat, the Torah says, *hitavu taava*. Literally, this can be taken to mean that they desired to desire.[6] The manna, he explains, may have tasted like anything one wanted, but eating it was a very different experience from all eating that we know. The manna was spiritual food; it lacked the properties of foodstuffs we are familiar with. Consuming it did

---

2. *Mekhilta, Beshallah, Vayisa, parasha* 2, s.v. *vayomer Hashem.*
3. Mishna Avot 6:4.
4. Berakhot 63b.
5. Num. 11:4.
6. The *Shev Shemateta* in his introduction (letters *zayin* and *het*) cites this thought in the name of the Alsheikh and fully develops it.

not stimulate any physical desire whatsoever. Those who complained yearned for their previous existence, when food delighted the senses and aroused them to eagerly look toward their next nibble. When the *Mekhilta* says that Torah was given only to manna eaters, it means that those who first received it had to live on a plane in which it did not have to compete with the pursuit of physical pleasures and delights. Those who threw themselves into its study in that first generation needed to be free of the desires that animate the rest of us.

We haven't been privileged to eat heavenly food for well over three millennia, nor can we delude ourselves regarding our complex desires. We understand just how important they are to us and how they wield enormous influence upon our behavior. We are expected, however, to control these desires. That is where the Shavuot offering comes in.

Bread stands as a symbol for two kinds of human need. Bread easily works as a code word for our greater sustenance. It also, however, serves as a euphemism for a very different need. When Yosef attempted to reason with his seductress, he spoke of the great trust his master Potiphar had shown toward him. Nothing in his household had been held back from Yosef's supervision, save for "the bread that he ate,"[7] a polite reference to Potiphar's wife. The two loaves of bread in the offering brought on Shavuot stand for these two desires that grip us so strongly.

How does the devoted servant of God deal with the desires that often interfere with his goodness and certainly with his focus on higher pursuits? One strategy that comes to mind is limiting and curtailing them. The more spiritually oriented personality will train himself to get by with simpler needs; he will shun any involvement with them that is unseemly.

While this approach seems obvious, people on a higher spiritual plane can do better. They can take their desires and their objects and elevate them. Rather than crush or hide them, a person can turn them into pure spirituality. (Think *korbanot*: atonement is won for the owner of an offering by the offering's consumption by the priests.)

This second, higher option is not an alternative open to everyone. Having just escaped the clutches of that fatal, fiftieth level of degradation, the Jews who left Egypt were not able to employ it. They needed a

---

7. Rashi on Gen. 39:6.

strong dose of taming their inner wants and desires, of learning to limit and do without. That process is expressed by the search for and destruction of *ḥametz*, the symbol of the flaws within us that are induced by the evil inclination.

After seven weeks of successfully curbing our baser instincts, we were ready for something more – for a new kind of offering to God, literally, a new *minḥa*. Our *avoda* was no longer symbolized by banishing *ḥametz*, but by elevating it.

This newness – the ability to sanctify and elevate, and not merely to discipline and curb – is the essence of the fiftieth day we count toward from the second day of Passover. We engage in self-elevation throughout the *sefira* period; if successful, we find ourselves positioned as elevated souls who can elevate the ordinary materials around us.

It is therefore not surprising at all that Shavuot, of all holidays, is the one that halakhically demands that we incorporate earthly pleasures like eating and drinking.[8] Initially, we regard this as counterintuitive. If anything, Shavuot is a holiday in which the very lack of any special mitzva to perform suggests that it is a time for spiritual contemplation and inner service. Even if the pleasures of the world are incorporated in other holidays, we would have thought that Shavuot is the exception. Instead, we learn that according to one opinion,[9] all holidays offer a choice of *avoda* – if a person chooses, he can spend his time in more spiritual pursuits and eschew any special holiday meals and the like – all holidays, that is, with the exception of Shavuot, where the merriment is mandatory.

We can now understand the reason. The embrace of the physical is not a concession to our lesser, physical selves but an affirmation of the elevation that we have gained in the seven weeks since Passover and of the specialness of the fiftieth day, which contains within it all the gains of the previous forty-nine.

As elevated people, we can and must practice on Shavuot our new skill of raising high everything around us, making that a key part of our *avoda*.

---

8. Pesaḥim 68b.
9. Albeit one that is not halakhically accepted.

Tisha B'Av

Rebuilding through Mourning

We don't travel down memory lane for the memories. At least as a national exercise, we do not revisit the past unless it has a bearing on the present and future.

Why, then, the elaborate buildup over the space of three weeks toward Tisha B'Av, seemingly for the purpose of getting us to more tearfully remember the past? Furthermore, our Sages tell us[1] that God decreed upon each deceased person that he should, in time, be forgotten. Yet, regarding the destruction of the Temple and Jerusalem, the verse proclaims[2] "If I forget Jerusalem, let my right hand forget its skill." After some two thousand years, we urge ourselves to remember, to not let go.

The inescapable conclusion we must reach is that we forget only the dead, while Jerusalem is very much alive. The essence of the Three Weeks is to be stubborn and obstinate, to refuse to accept the destruction of Jerusalem. We cannot achieve "closure," not after all the centuries

---

Based on *Netivot Shalom*, Numbers, 190–192.
1. See Soferim, *hosafa* 1, 1:3.
2. Ps. 137:5.

that have passed, because we cannot come to terms with life without the Temple.

A man unburdened himself to the Apter Rebbe, reciting his list of personal tragedies and failures. Somewhere in the conversation, he sensed that the Rav did not show sufficient signs of commiserating with him. Noting his dissatisfaction, the Rav explained. "I see that you are deeply pained by your circumstances. Tell me, what about the *korban tamid*, the daily offering in the Temple, that was not brought this morning? Are you also pained by that?"

Two thousand years after the last *korban tamid* was brought, the Apter Rebbe could not understand that another Jew might not be disconsolate regarding our inability to properly perform the offerings of the Temple. In his reaction, we get to the heart of our *avoda* during the Three Weeks. The single most important ingredient is refusing to accept "reality." We cannot and should not make peace with the loss of the Temple.

Our longing for the Temple is transformed into a kind of offering, as if the Temple stood and we participated in its service. Ironically, without a *Beit HaMikdash*, we can still offer *korbanot* – the offerings of shattered hearts, pining for reconnection with the *Shekhina*. (Longing for something can sometimes be more valuable than attaining it.) This longing for the Temple is an important component of its rebuilding. The Three Weeks, our focused longing for the Temple, amounts to the beginning of its reconstruction.

Our mourning differs from the way others mourn. Rabbi Meir Chodosh saw an allusion to this in the Torah's description of the infant Moshe: "She opened it [the basket that bore Moshe] and saw the child, and behold, a youth was crying. She took pity on him, and said, 'This is one of the Hebrew boys.'"[3] From his crying, Pharaoh's daughter understood that the baby was Jewish, because Jewish crying is different from others. Most crying comes from a sense of rupture, hopelessness, and often despair. Jewish crying is forward-looking and is rooted in longing and hope for the future. (For this reason, many Holocaust victims were

---

3. Ex. 2:6.

unable to cry. Having given up any hope for the future, they were not able to cry in the Jewish way they were accustomed to.)

A teaching of the Baal Shem Tov highlights the value of our mourning. Between (in a manner of speaking) our world and God's, there are numerous "worlds" that bridge the distance. Many of us are familiar with the names of some of these conceptual worlds, like *atzilut, beria,* and *yetzira.* Among these worlds is one so rarified and lofty that nothing connected to physicality in any manner or form can penetrate.

When we pray, we send our prayers aloft, launching them on what we hope will be the shortest trajectory to God's heavenly throne. When they reach this particular world, taught the Baal Shem Tov, they hit a barrier. Our prayers, after all, are distilled into words. Words are products of human speech, of physical beings. Words still belong in our imperfect world, not in this lofty place to which we send them.

Only one kind of praying makes it into that world. One element makes its way through the barrier: our *kavana,* the earnest feeling and sentiment of our hearts, completely divorced from any limiting agents like mere words. This inner will, this spiritual essence, fits right into that world. If the words of prayer are like a body, their inner essence is its soul. Souls, indeed, are welcome in that world. (On the other hand, in that particular world, words that spring more from the lips than the heart have no value. It is not that they count as something, albeit less than they would if said with *kavana.* There, the words alone count for nothing at all. *Kavana* is the only currency accepted. Without it, the prayers have no meaning at all.)

In the physical world that we consciously inhabit, our contemporary *avoda* during the Three Weeks makes perfect sense. Even the sacrificial offerings have a physical side to them. They all utilize objects and elements of the world around us. Our sincere longing for closeness to God, however, does not come from a physical place. It can penetrate that higher, esoteric world and take its place there. The destruction of the Temple did not close the gate on this kind of service to God. In that world, the *avoda* of the *Beit HaMikdash* is still feasible. We perform it entirely from within; our *korban* is the sadness, the longing that grows out of our having been separated from the immediate presence of our Creator.

There is an oblique reference to that lofty world in the Gemara,[4] which describes a "place" in heaven where mourning does not reach. That place is the world we have been describing, where the *avoda* of our broken hearts accomplishes its task in the same way that *korbanot* did when the Temple operated in Jerusalem.

While the Temple stood, it was used by people who could long and yearn for those special sweet moments of the year when they were touched by direct contact with the *Shekhina*. Jews of those times powerfully felt the general aura of holiness brought by the Divine Presence in the land and in their midst. How they must have yearned for even more and greater closeness!

But ironically, in one sense, the destruction of the physical *Beit HaMikdash* had a positive impact on the quality of our *avoda*. We know of only separation and distance. We have only our imagination to use, to gain some inkling of what it was like. We are capable of an intense longing and yearning born of centuries of deprivation since the Temple's destruction. Similarly, the destruction initiated great longing within God, as it were, to bring about reconciliation with His people and return His *Shekhina* to its appointed abode in Jerusalem.

This longing paves the way for the rebuilding of the *Beit HaMikdash*. Our mourning for the Temple is thus a powerful factor in its reconstruction – it is the mortar binding together the stones of the future one. There is wonderful irony in this, and great hope; as we enter the Three Weeks each year, it is also a challenge.

---

4. Ḥagiga 5b. The reference is puzzling. While the Gemara does say that in this world there is no crying, it also says that mourning for the destruction of the Temple is the exception and does take place there.

The Three Weeks: Kernel of Rebirth

C hildren delight in learning that all living things begin with some tiny seed. For children, this is a wondrous discovery. Adults might be better prepared to handle the full truth, even though it includes part of the story that is not so romantic but profound nonetheless.

The road from seed to new life travels through a neighborhood on the wrong side of the tracks. Living things actually begin with decay. Every seed must disintegrate before it participates in a spurt of growth. Within every small seed is an even smaller essence, surrounded by supporting material that wastes away before this *kusta deḥiyuta* – the vital kernel – begins its dramatic ascent.[1]

It should not seem so strange then that the process of destruction could and does generate a precious remainder, the basic matter upon which rebuilding is ultimately based. This is the way of the natural world. It is also part of our history. Before our redemption in Egypt, we

---

Based on *Netivot Shalom*, Numbers, 193–195.

1. In other words, it is not so much that big oaks from little acorns grow, as big oaks from decayed acorns emerge.

lost spiritual ground, slipping so badly that we descended to the forty-ninth level of impurity, sinking to a nadir of decay and emptiness. The redemption came from within that void.

This holds true in the lives of individuals as well. The prophet Micah wrote,[2] "Although I fell, I arose; although I dwell in darkness, Hashem is my light." The *Yalkut Shimoni*[3] adds, "From within the falling is the rising; within the darkness there is light."

All these sources tell a similar story: the solution is born within the problem itself.

In regard to the Temple, the "vital kernel" that activates the growth of the next Temple is the Jewish people's mourning for the last one. The cries of hope and longing lead directly to the next *Beit HaMikdash*.

In truth, they lead to much more. The coming of the Messiah is itself contingent on the belief and expectation of his arrival. Without our yearly exercise in understanding what we have lost, in pitying ourselves for the hollowness inside that results from our being deprived of Hashem's closeness, we would become inured to our condition and forget what we ought to be looking toward. The evil inclination to divert our attention from the Temple is unusually potent, because so much depends on our proper focus, including our long-awaited redemption.

It is a mistake to think of our practices leading up to Tisha B'Av as mere "customs." They are part of a coordinated plan to rivet our attention on our loss and to shore up our *emuna* and confidence in the future. As such, they are nothing less than facilitators of the arrival of the Messiah.

The end of history also follows this pattern. Just before the covers in front of the light of the Messiah are removed, we will experience a terrible period of catastrophic darkness in the period we know as *ikveta demeshiha*, the time preceding the arrival of the Messiah. We have already seen terrible pain, the horrors of the Holocaust, and a precipitous erosion of our spirituality. This collapse of Jewish life as we once knew it in its depth and glory also releases a vital essence

---

2. Micah 7:8.
3. *Yalkut Shimoni, Ekev* 852, s.v. *kum reid.*

that can grow into something new and better. Disintegration precedes rebuilding once more.

Yet for all its effectiveness, stewing in the misery of mourning seems wrong. Ordinarily, the hardest *kelipa*, the toughest barrier between ourselves and genuine spirituality, is sorrow and depression. Addressing this, the *Peri Haaretz* cites a midrash[4] that comments on the words of Lamentations:[5] "Hashem has afflicted her for her abundant transgressions." The midrash adds, "I might suppose that for naught. Therefore the verse teaches, 'for her abundant transgressions.'" The *Peri Haaretz* explains that "for naught" refers to our mourning. We might think that we shed tears and lament for a Temple in the distant past that will not be reclaimed through our sorrow. Such crying is indeed for naught. But this is not the case. We mourn not for the past, but for our sorry state, when we behold the abundance of our transgressions, without which a new Temple would have long ago been built.

Moreover, our faults do double duty in the tragedy arena. On a national level, they are responsible for the continuation of our long exile, for obstructing the righting of the toppled stones of our Temple. And although individually each of us is a small *Beit HaMikdash*, ready to receive the enlightenment of the *Shekhina*, we find our inner sanctuaries in a state of ruin, devoid of the Divine Spirit that should inhabit them. This, too, owes to an abundance of transgressions, giving us good reason to mourn.

Our mourning leaves us shattered and broken. But dismantling the fortresses of our egos can be healthy. We can recognize why we feel broken – and begin to do something about it. If we are distant from God because of what we have done, not because of what we are, we can address the problem responsibly through repentance. Thus, taught Rabbi Pinḥas Koretzer, Tisha B'Av observed properly brings about atonement. Furthermore, he said, we gain from it yearlong. Just as we draw joy for an entire year from Sukkot, the holiday of rejoicing, so too we feel a healthy, therapeutic brokenness due to Tisha B'Av.

---

4. Lamentations Rabba 33:1.
5. Lam. 1:5.

"All her pursuers caught up with her *bein hametzarim*."[6] The Maggid of Mezeritch detected something positive in this image. A king must usually maintain a distance from every ordinary subject. Not everyone is freely admitted to the court. The rules change when the king travels, when he is away from the palace. Those who encounter him on the road have much freer access. Similarly, the Maggid of Mezeritch taught, the Three Weeks offer us a time to catch up with the King, to enter His presence even when we have failed to do so during the rest of the year. This would make little sense if our mourning focused on the past alone. Recalling a spiritually glorious past will not bring a person closer to God.

In the case of the Temple, this vital core is our mourning, our pain and longing for the connection to God we once enjoyed. When our mind's eye grasps an image of the Temple Mount after the destruction of the Temple, we see only broken stones and charred beams. We do not realize that we are also looking at the beginnings of its renewal. The destruction cut a gaping hole into our hearts. Every time we feel its pain, every year that we continue to mourn and refuse to be resigned to the past, we contribute directly to the reconstruction.

Tisha B'Av, then, is an all-important link between the past and the glory to be of the Messiah. Were it not for Tisha B'Av, we could, in time, be cut off from the past and thereby squander our opportunity for the future. Left to our own leanings and the evil inclination, we might be resigned to the events of the past. Our Sages cleverly prevented this from happening by creating the period of the Three Weeks, ensuring that old wound will never fully close. The Three Weeks should be seen not simply as a season of assorted practices. Rather, it is the vehicle through which we not only keep alive the commitment regarding the Messiah that "I will wait for him each day" but also nurture the nascent regrowth of redemption that emerged from the ruins of destruction.

---

6. Lam. 1:3. The phrase *bein hametzarim* literally means "in dire straits." It also alludes to the three weeks of mourning between the two fast days – *Shiva Asar BeTammuz* and Tisha B'Av – marking the final phase in the destruction of Jerusalem.

Tisha B'Av as a Holiday

There was no Jewish holiday like the day the Temple was destroyed."[1] Holiday? We struggle to find a bit of consolation on our national day of mourning for the loss of the *Beit HaMikdash* and the endless succession of horrors and outrages that have befallen us as a people. How can we possibly call it a holiday?

But it is indeed. The very despair of Tisha B'Av yields dividends that are cause for celebration.

Who wins the favor of the king? The easiest example we could find is that of a beloved prince, whose every accomplishment and talent reflect positively on his father, and who therefore brings him much honor.

Ironically, however, someone who brings the king no honor at all may win more of the king's love. Should the prince be mentally disabled, he will arouse powerful feelings of closeness in the king. Realizing that

---

Based on *Netivot Shalom, Bemidbar*, 196–199.

1. Midrash cited by *Ohev Yisrael, Deuteronomy, Shabbat Ḥazon*, s.v. *yesh lomar asher*. The midrash applies this thought to Lamentations 1:15, "He proclaimed a *moed* against me." According to the plain meaning of the verse, *moed* is understood to mean a set time, i.e., God appointed a set time to visit His destruction upon us. However, the midrash takes note of the fact that *moed* also has the specific connotation of a holiday, a set time for rejoicing.

his son cannot look out for himself and depends completely upon his father for protection and care, the king is overwhelmed by compassion. Here is the parallel to Tisha B'Av. We reached the nadir of our national existence when we forced the Divine Presence to withdraw from its chosen abode. Our complete helplessness leads to feelings of compassion in God, as it were, that surpass those on the days we usually think of as holidays.

The Torah calls us *banim*, children, of God. Fatherly love comes in different forms. The most obvious is the love shared at close range. Separate the father from the son and the love is now compounded by yearning, by the gnawing pain of distance. If we push further yet, we can detect another variety of love still stronger than the others. Imagine a child who is deathly ill and desperately in need of surgery. The father is a surgeon, and only he can save the child. The cries of the child pierce his heart. When he places the blade of the scalpel against the tender skin of the child, the parent might as well be cutting into his own flesh. The love that the father feels at that moment is the strongest of all his contradictory and tempestuous emotions. Seeing the child with his life in peril, realizing his utter helplessness save for the intervention of the father – these produce a love beyond that which is aroused in other situations.

This is Tisha B'Av, and this is why our Sages call it a holiday. Indeed, it is a "holiday" like no other. The love of God for the Jewish people is without condition and without bounds. In our moment of greatest weakness, greatest vulnerability, and greatest distance from Him, the compassion of our Father is moved as on no other day.

He displayed this love through the embrace of the *Keruvim*,[2] the golden cherubs atop the Ark, which the enemy took note of and mocked. That embrace was paradoxical. Our Sages tell us[3] that the orientation of the *Keruvim* depended on how well the Jewish people obeyed the will of the Creator. When the Jewish people hearkened to God's voice, the *Keruvim* turned toward each other in a sign of mutual love. When the Jewish people disobeyed, the *Keruvim* turned away from each other. The embrace of the *Keruvim* at the time of the destruction is therefore

---

2. Yoma 54b.
3. Bava Batra 99a.

surprising. We would have expected God to display separation and distance at that terrible moment. The embrace of the *Keruvim* offered a different message: the abiding love and longing of a Father for His people.

An entirely different argument explains the holiday-like character of Tisha B'Av from another perspective. We find very little spiritual consistency in our world. Not all places and times are created equal. To the contrary, they all appear very different. We have no trouble isolating places that are holier than others – including ten different levels of holiness within the Land of Israel. On the other hand, Egypt is seen by our Sages as *ervat haaretz*, or the most debased and spiritually deprived place on earth. Similarly, holiness distributes itself unequally over time. There are times of average holiness, greater holiness, and greatest holiness. These distinctions are all for our good. If they were not, they would not exist.

We can readily understand at least one of the dividends of a world of changing potential for holiness. We try to take advantage of the opportunity that the special days of the year offer us. We push ourselves to anticipate them, to prepare for them, and to act differently on them. Contemplate the value of attaching ourselves to God not on the special days of the year, but on the ordinary ones. Then consider the value of doing the same at times that we are particularly distant from God. Swimming against the spiritual current is a most powerful exercise!

Now consider what transpired at the time of the destruction of the Temple. Jews became aware that enemy soldiers were not only on the Temple Mount but had entered the Holy of Holies. Ordinarily, only the High Priest would enter and only on Yom Kippur after elaborate preparation and as part of a complex *avoda*. Yet now the enemy impudently entered and defiled it, mocking the Temple, its people, and its God.

No greater insult to national pride could be contemplated. Their personal despair was now compounded by national disgrace and degradation. All who understood what had happened became tortured, broken souls. Those souls still longed for God, wanted desperately to feel close again, even though – or because – they sensed that they had fallen into a spiritual pit.

God cherishes the soul that is broken and turns to Him in its pain. He reacted to a nation of broken souls by displaying the *Keruvim* locked in embrace, as if at a time of great closeness. And indeed it was. The Jewish people's yearning for Him when He appeared distant led to His reasserting His commitment to them. This is the stuff a *moed* is made of. (The word literally means a time of special encounter and discovery.) Tisha B'Av was indeed a holiday.

It is no coincidence that the Torah reading for the first Shabbat in the Three Weeks is *Parashat Pinḥas*, which contains the special Temple offerings for all the holidays of the year.

This quality of *moed* regarding Tisha B'Av expresses itself in several ways. Kabbalistic literature calls our attention to a remarkable identity. The most concentrated holiday season we know occurs in Tishrei. Altogether, there are twenty-two days from Rosh HaShana until the end of the Tishrei holiday period. The same number of days form the period of mourning for the Temple, between *Shiva Asar BeTammuz* and Tisha B'Av.

This is not coincidental, say the kabbalistic works. It was meant to be. Once we grasp the notion that Tisha B'Av has features of a *moed* we are better prepared to accept that the parallels between these periods are not coincidental but deliberate; the two periods are actually closely related. The next step is still a bit of a shock.

If the periods are parallel, then each day in the Tammuz-Av period is paired with one in Tishrei. Tisha B'Av – the last day of the summer period of twenty-two days – is matched with Simḥat Torah, the final day of the Tishrei holiday period. The joy of Simḥat Torah, through which we sing and dance our way to an affirmation of our love of God's Torah, has a parallel in Tisha B'Av. In the midst of their despair and darkness – or more accurately, because of it – Jews learned on that day that God's love for them was unending and unyielding. They understood that God was still with them no less than when they merited His closeness by living according to His commandments.

Are we then to turn Tisha B'Av into a joyous occasion? Of course not. But the idea we have developed modifies our practical *avoda* on that day. Consider the contrast between two of the great sages in Ḥasidut. The Saba Kadisha would fall to the ground at the day's beginning, weeping with outstretched limbs and continuing to weep this way the entire day. (A doctor who observed this remarked that he had thought it humanly impossible for a person to cry so much.) The Maggid of Kozhnitz, by contrast, would occupy his day with inspiring words that fortified one spiritually, banishing the fog of gloom and desperation that can easily lead people to paralysis in their *avoda*.

One of his own parables helps explain his behavior. A small but elite group of musicians was kept in the employ of a king. They weren't called upon too often, at least not when things were going well. But when the world began to weigh heavily upon the king and he began descending toward melancholy, they sprang into action to cheer him up.

On Tisha B'Av, said the Maggid of Kozhnitz, the King's heart is heavy. All those who love Him will want to gladden the heart of the King who followed His people into exile.

It seems that the Maggid must have been a member of God's special elite group. Other Jews have to figure out their place, each one according to who he is. While all must mourn, we must also find within our *avoda* a way to go beyond the mourning. For some, it will be in the form of resisting the natural tendency to become depressed and crushed. For others, it will be a reaffirmation of God's kingship, expressing undying loyalty and devotion to Him even at the worst of times.

Glossary

afikoman: the matza that is eaten at the end of the Passover Seder.

ahava: love.

Akeda: literally, "binding." The attempted offering of Yitzḥak at God's command to Avraham.

arayot: forbidden relations.

avoda: service; sometimes used as a truncated form of *avodat Hashem*, service of God.

Beit HaMikdash: the Temple.

Benei Yisrael: the Children of Israel.

bikkurim: first fruits, brought to the Temple as an offering.

bitaḥon: trust.

bittul: negation.

daat: understanding. Sometimes refers to the *sefira* of the same name, in which case it indicates the cosmic source of understanding.

devekut: the state of utter attachment of a human soul to God.

din: judgment; see also *gevura*.

Ein Sof: Infinite One; a kabbalistic term for God's most remote aspects.

Elokut: Divinity.

emuna: belief, especially in God.

epha: a biblical measure.

eved: servant or slave.

Gan Eden: the Garden of Eden.

gematria: the process of noting the connection between words and phrases based on their numerical value. (Each Hebrew letter has a number equivalent.)

gevura: strength. When used in references to the *sefirot,* it connotes those that show restraint. It is inwardly focused, in contrast to *ḥesed,* which is expansive, focusing outwardly on some recipient. *Gevura* is integrally connected with *din,* judgment, because it sets boundaries and limits.

Haggada: the mitzva of retelling the story of the Exodus on the first night of Passover. It also refers to the traditional text used to guide the Seder on the night of Passover.

hakafot: festive circuits in the synagogue with the Torah scrolls on Simḥat Torah.

halakha (pl. **halakhot**): Jewish law.

Hallel: a prayer of enthusiastic praise of God recited on festive days, composed of passages from Psalms.

ḥametz: leaven, forbidden on Passover.

Hasid: one who acts superlatively, exceeding the requirements of righteousness.

ḥattat: a type of sin-offering brought in the Temple.

ḥesed (pl. **ḥasadim**): lovingkindness.

hester panim: hiding of the divine countenance, where God seems to become unresponsive to human entreaties.

ḥitzonim: literally, "externalities." Negative or neutral forces that encase, as it were, some of the latent holiness of this world, and obscure its light and purpose.

ḥokhma wisdom.

Hoshanot: special prayers of supplication recited during the circuits of the *bima* on Sukkot and Hoshana Rabba.

ikveta demeshiḥa: literally, "the footsteps of the Messiah," i.e., the period of time immediately before the arrival of the Messiah.

itaruta dele'eila: arousing, or awakening, from Above; God's precipitating a spiritual response in man through some action of His.

itaruta deletata: arousing, or awakening, from below; man's precipitating a spiritual response in himself through his own initiative.

kavana: focus and concentration.

kedusha: holiness.

kelipa: literally, "shell." A covering that surrounds and is impervious to holiness, not allowing entrance to the holiness that could otherwise penetrate.

Keruvim: the cherubs atop the Ark.

keter: literally, "crown." The highest element in the hierarchy of *sefirot*, often understood as standing above the ten.

Klal Yisrael: the collective identity of Israel; the Jewish people as a whole.

Knesset Yisrael: the mystical entity that is the collective soul of the Jewish people.

korban (pl. *korbanot*): Temple offering.

maḥzor: the holiday prayer book.

malkhut: literally, kingship. When used in the context of the *sefirot*, it refers to the lowest of the ten, distributing its accumulated spiritual energies to their appropriate recipients, just as a beneficent king does to his subjects.

mesirut nefesh: self-sacrifice.

midda (pl. *middot*): a personality trait, like arrogance, humility, anger, or zeal. In reference to God, it can sometimes refer to one of the *sefirot*.

midrash: exegetical commentary; uncovering layers of meaning in a text beyond the plain meaning. The word also often refers to a particular collection of such commentary.

minḥa: a flour-offering in the Temple; it also refers to the afternoon prayer.

mishloaḥ manot: the sending of food gifts to friends, one of the halakhic requirements on Purim.

moed (pl. *moadim*): appointed time; holiday.

Musaf: the additional prayer service added on Shabbat and holidays.

musar: the Torah teachings dealing with character formation and ethical behavior.

nega'im: plagues; discolorations of houses, garments, and skin treated as signs of heavenly displeasure.

neshama (pl. *neshamot*): soul.

nesi'im: the princes of the tribes of Israel.

Omer: a biblical measure; usually used to identify the offering of new barley on the second day of Passover.

parasha (pl. *parashot*): section of text, often referring to the section that is the designated Torah reading of the week.

reshut: permissible, but not mandatory.

ruaḥ hakodesh: a spirit of divine assistance that extends a person's understanding and capability beyond typical boundaries.

Sefirat HaOmer: the counting of the Omer, i.e., the counting of fifty days between the second day of Passover and Shavuot.

sefirot (sing. *sefira*): the "attributes" of God that govern how the infinity of God expresses itself in the spiritual and physical worlds. They are a key concept in Kabbala.

Shas: an acronym for *shisha sidrei*, the six orders (of Mishna), in other words, the whole of the Talmud.

Sheheḥeyanu: "Who has sustained us in life"; a blessing made on special, periodic occasions.

Shekhina: the Divine Presence.

Shema: a section of the Torah, recited twice each day, that is the traditional declaration of Jewish faith.

Shemitta: the Sabbatical year, in which the land may not be worked, that which grows on its own is shared by all, and debts are canceled.

Shemoneh Esreh: literally, "eighteen." The *Amida*, the central text of the daily mandated prayer service, which originally included eighteen blessings (a nineteenth was later added).

shira: song, particularly ecstatic praise of God upon a momentous occasion.

Shulḥan Arukh: the Code of Jewish Law (sixteenth century).

simḥa: happiness; rejoicing; joy.

Sitra Aḥra: literally, "the other side." In order to maintain man's free choice, neither good nor evil can prevail cosmically. All the good that God created must be offset by forces of evil coming from "the other side" in order to keep good and evil in a state of balance, affording man the opportunity to choose between equally compelling alternatives.

taava: desire; lust.

tahara: purity.

tahor: spiritually pure.

tamid: the daily mandatory communal offering in the Temple.

terua: a shofar sounding composed of a series of short blasts.

teshuva : repentance.

tiferet: the third of the lower seven *sefirot*, seen as a combination of ḥesed and *gevura*, and often associated with Yaakov and with Torah.

tikkun: literally, "rectification" or "remedy." Getting to the goal of Creation requires first undoing the imperfection introduced by man's election of evil.

tuma: spiritual impurity.

tzaddik: righteous person.

tzedaka: charitable contribution.

Ushpizin: literally, "guests," referring to the seven biblical shepherds of our people and the *sefirot* they represent.

Yiddishkeit: (Yiddish) Judaism.

yira: fear or reverence.

The fonts used in this book are from the Arno family